San Francisco, California Travel Guide 2024-2025

Insider Tips, Hidden Gems, and Must-See Spots for your Trip to the City by the Bay

Evelyn Blair

Copyright © 2024 by Evelyn Blair

All rights reserved. No part of this book may be reproduced, distributed, or transmitted in any form or by any means, including photocopying, recording, or other electronic or mechanical methods, without the prior written permission of the publisher, except in the case of brief quotations embodied in critical reviews and certain other noncommercial uses permitted by copyright law.

This guide is intended for informational purposes only. While every effort has been made to ensure the accuracy of the information provided, the publisher and author disclaims any liability for any loss, injury, or inconvenience sustained by any person using this guide.

All rights reserved. No part of this publication may be reproduced, stored in a retrieval system, or transmitted, in any form or by any means, without the prior written permission of the publisher.

Map of San Francisco

Scan the qr code to see the map of San Francisco

3

Table of Contents

INTRODUCTION	**8**
Discovering San Francisco	10
How to Use This Guide	13
A Brief History of San Francisco	17
CHAPTER 1	**20**
Planning Your Trip	**20**
CHAPTER 2	**36**
Neighbourhoods	**36**
Union Square	36
Chinatown	40
North Beach	43
Financial District	46
Nob Hill	49
Russian Hill	52
Fisherman's Wharf	55
Marina District	58
Pacific Heights	61
Haight-Ashbury	64
Castro	67
Mission District	70
South of Market (SoMa)	73
Tenderloin	76
Hayes Valley	79
Japantown	82

Presidio	85
Richmond District	88
Sunset District	91
Noe Valley	94
Bernal Heights	97
Glen Park	100
Excelsior District	103
Bayview-Hunters Point	106
Twin Peaks	109
CHAPTER 3	**113**
Getting There And Around	**113**
CHAPTER 4	**133**
Accomodations	**133**
Luxury Hotels	133
Boutique Hotels	139
Budget-Friendly Accommodations	144
Hostels	147
Vacation Rentals	151
Family-Friendly Accommodations	155
The Best Neighbourhoods to Stay in	160
CHAPTER 5	**165**
Top Attractions	**165**
Golden Gate Bridge	165
Alcatraz Island	169
Fisherman's Wharf	172
Pier 39	175
Golden Gate Park	179
The Painted Ladies	183
San Francisco's Chinatown	185

Lombard Street	188
San Francisco Museum of Modern Art (SFMOMA)	191
The Exploratorium	194
The Presidio	197
Coit Tower	199
CHAPTER 6	**203**
Hidden Gems	**203**
Mission District Murals	203
Wave Organ	206
Sutro Baths	209
Lands End	212
Filbert Steps	215
Baker Beach	218
CHAPTER 7	**221**
Activities for Different Travellers	**221**
Activities for Solo Travelers	221
Activities for Couples	223
Family-Friendly Activities	225
CHAPTER 8	**228**
Outdoor Activities	**228**
Hiking Trails	228
Beaches	230
Parks and Gardens	233
Biking Routes	236
Water Sports	239
CHAPTER 9	**243**
For Kids	**243**
CHAPTER 10	**249**
Culinary Delights and Nightlife	**249**

Dishes	249
Fine Dining	253
Casual Dining	258
Budget-Friendly Dining	262
Street Food	266
Cafes and Bakeries	269
Bars And Pubs	274
Nightclubs and Live Music Venues	278
Wine Bars and Breweries	283
CHAPTER 11	**287**
Shopping	**287**
CHAPTER 12	**293**
Cultural Experiences	**293**
Festivals and Events	293
Performing Arts	296
Art Galleries	299
Historic Sites and Landmarks	303
Religious and Spiritual Sites	307
CHAPTER 13	**310**
Day Trips	**310**
PRACTICAL INFORMATION AND TIPS	**314**
BONUS	**319**
A 4-Day Itinerary for Seeing San Francisco	**319**
CONCLUSION	**324**

INTRODUCTION

Traveling to San Francisco can be overwhelming with its many attractions, diverse neighborhoods, and unique cultural nuances. It's easy to feel lost and miss out on the best experiences this vibrant city has to offer. Without the right guidance, you might spend your time navigating tourist traps instead of discovering the true essence of San Francisco.

This book offers a solution by providing all the information you need to explore San Francisco confidently and enjoyably. It covers everything from iconic landmarks like the Golden Gate Bridge and Alcatraz to hidden gems in lesser-known neighborhoods. This guide is designed to help you make the most of your visit.

Drawing on extensive research and insights, this guide ensures you have the most accurate and valuable recommendations. The information in this book is curated to give you the best possible experience.

By using this book, you'll save time and avoid common tourist pitfalls. Instead of wandering aimlessly or following generic advice, you'll have a well-planned itinerary that highlights the best of San Francisco. Readers would transform their trips into unforgettable experiences with this advice, seeing places they never would have found on their own.

By the end of this book, you'll not only have a fantastic itinerary but also feel like you truly understand and appreciate the vibrant spirit of San Francisco. Knowing you have the best recommendations will give you the confidence to explore for yourself.

Don't wait until you're overwhelmed and confused in the middle of your trip. Start planning now to ensure you don't miss out on the incredible opportunities San Francisco has to offer. Dive into the pages ahead to uncover the secrets of this fascinating city and embark on an amazing journey. Happy travels, and enjoy every moment in San Francisco.

Discovering San Francisco

San Francisco is a city filled with rich history, beautiful scenery, and a unique culture. Located on the West Coast of the United States, it sits on a peninsula surrounded by the Pacific Ocean and San Francisco Bay. This city is known for its iconic landmarks, diverse neighborhoods, and vibrant atmosphere. As you explore San Francisco, you'll find that it has something for everyone, from breathtaking natural beauty to impressive man-made wonders.

One of the first things you'll notice about San Francisco is its famous hills. The city is built on more than 40 hills, providing stunning views from almost every corner. The steep streets can be challenging to walk, but they also offer incredible vistas of the city and the water. The most famous hill, Twin Peaks, offers a panoramic view of the entire city, making it a must-visit spot for anyone looking to capture the beauty of San Francisco.

The Golden Gate Bridge is another highlight of San Francisco. This bright red suspension bridge spans the Golden Gate Strait, connecting the city to Marin County. It is one of the most photographed landmarks in the world, and walking or biking across it is a popular activity for visitors. The bridge is not only an engineering marvel but also a symbol of the city's innovation and resilience.

San Francisco is also home to Alcatraz Island, a small island located in the middle of San Francisco Bay.

Alcatraz was once a federal prison that housed some of America's most notorious criminals. Today, it is a national park and a major tourist attraction. Visitors can take a ferry to the island and explore the historic prison, learning about its fascinating history through guided tours and exhibits.

The city's neighborhoods each have their own unique charm and character. Chinatown is the oldest and one of the largest Chinese communities outside of Asia. It is a bustling area filled with shops, restaurants, and markets, offering a glimpse into Chinese culture and traditions. The Mission District, known for its colorful murals and vibrant Latino community, is another area worth exploring. Here, you can enjoy delicious food, lively music, and beautiful street art.

San Francisco's waterfront is another major draw for visitors. Fisherman's Wharf is a lively area where you can enjoy fresh seafood, visit souvenir shops, and watch sea lions lounging at Pier 39. The Ferry Building Marketplace, located at the foot of Market Street, is a great place to sample local foods and shop for artisanal products. Walking along the Embarcadero, you can take in the sights and sounds of the bustling waterfront.

Golden Gate Park is an expansive green space in the heart of the city, offering a peaceful escape from the urban hustle. The park is home to several attractions, including the California Academy of Sciences, the de Young Museum, and the Japanese Tea Garden. Whether you're interested in science, art, or simply enjoying nature, the park has something to offer.

San Francisco is also known for its diverse and innovative food scene. The city offers a wide range of dining options, from high-end restaurants to casual eateries. Seafood is a highlight, with dishes like clam chowder in a sourdough bread bowl and Dungeness crab being local favorites. The city is also a hub for international cuisine, reflecting its multicultural population.

In addition to its attractions, San Francisco has a mild climate that makes it a great destination year-round. The city experiences cool summers and mild winters, with frequent fog that adds to its unique charm. Dressing in layers is recommended, as the weather can change quickly, especially near the water.

Exploring San Francisco is a rewarding experience, offering a mix of natural beauty, historic landmarks, and vibrant culture. Whether you're wandering through its picturesque neighborhoods, marveling at its iconic sights, or enjoying its culinary delights, San Francisco promises a memorable adventure.

How to Use This Guide

This guide is designed to help you explore and enjoy San Francisco to the fullest. To make the most of your visit, it is important to understand how to navigate the wealth of information provided here. This guide is structured to be easy to follow and packed with valuable insights, ensuring your trip is both enjoyable and memorable.

Start by familiarizing yourself with the layout of the guide. It is divided into sections that cover different aspects of your trip, from planning and logistics to the best attractions and activities. Each section provides detailed information, tips, and recommendations to help you make informed decisions. The table of contents at the beginning of the guide is your roadmap. It lists all the sections and chapters, allowing you to quickly find the information you need.

When planning your trip, begin with the sections on "Planning Your Trip," "Neighbourhoods," and "Getting There and Around." These chapters provide essential information on the best times to visit San Francisco, visa requirements, and how to get to the city. They also offer practical advice on transportation options within the city, helping you navigate San Francisco efficiently.

Once you have the basics covered, move on to "Accommodations." This section helps you find the perfect place to stay based on your preferences and budget. Whether you are looking for luxury hotels, budget-friendly options, or family-friendly accommodations, this guide offers comprehensive reviews and suggestions to meet your needs. To assist you further, website links have been provided for some hotels and restaurants. Clicking on these links will direct you to their official websites for more details and booking options.

With your accommodation sorted, delve into the heart of the guide: "Top Attractions" and "Hidden Gems." These chapters highlight the must-see landmarks and lesser-known spots that make San Francisco unique. Detailed descriptions and insider tips will help you plan your itinerary, ensuring you don't miss any of the city's iconic sights. Some images have been included to give you a visual preview of these attractions, making it easier to decide where to go.

As you explore, refer to the "Activities" section for ideas tailored to different interests and group sizes. This section offers suggestions for solo travelers, couples, families, and groups, ensuring everyone finds something they enjoy. From outdoor adventures to cultural experiences, the guide provides a diverse range of activities to suit all tastes.

Also, do well the check out the "For Kids" Section. It provides a range of activities and attractions that kids would love. Make use of the QR codes provided for the booking of some of the tickets.

Dining is a major part of any travel experience, and the "Culinary Delights and Nightlife" section is your go-to

14

resource for discovering San Francisco's vibrant food scene. This chapter covers everything from top restaurants to cozy cafes and lively bars. Recommendations include local favorites and hidden gems, ensuring you experience the best of San Francisco's culinary offerings. Website links are also provided for many dining establishments, allowing you to check menus, hours, and make reservations directly.

Shopping enthusiasts will find the "Shopping" section invaluable. It provides an overview of the best places to shop, from bustling markets to high-end boutiques. Detailed descriptions and tips help you discover unique items and souvenirs to bring home.

The "Cultural Experiences" section guides you through the city's rich cultural landscape. From festivals and events to museums and theaters, this chapter helps you immerse yourself in San Francisco's diverse cultural heritage. Recommendations for performances, exhibitions, and historic sites ensure a well-rounded cultural experience.

For those interested in exploring beyond the city, the "Day Trips" section offers suggestions for exciting excursions. Detailed itineraries and tips help you plan trips to nearby attractions like Napa Valley, Muir Woods, and more. These day trips provide a perfect break from city life and a chance to experience the natural beauty of the surrounding areas.

The "Practical Information and Tips" section is your guide to staying safe and well-prepared during your trip. It includes safety tips, health services, local etiquette, and emergency contacts. This chapter ensures you have all the necessary information to handle any situation that may arise. Also, a 4-day itinerary is provided for convenience.

To enhance your experience further, some parts of the book include QR codes. These codes can be scanned to access maps of certain places or to book tickets. Details are provided below each QR code for your convenience, do well to refer to them. To scan the QR codes, you can use a smartphone camera or a QR code scanning app available on most app stores.

Use this guide as your companion throughout your journey in San Francisco. Each section is crafted to provide you with the knowledge and confidence to explore the city like a local. Keep it handy, refer to it often, and let it guide you to an unforgettable San Francisco adventure.

A Brief History of San Francisco

San Francisco is a city with a rich and fascinating history that spans several centuries. The area was originally inhabited by the Ohlone people, who lived here for thousands of years before the arrival of Europeans. They thrived in this region, making use of the abundant natural resources provided by the bay and surrounding lands.

The first recorded European to visit the area was Spanish explorer Juan Bautista de Anza in 1776. He established the Presidio of San Francisco, a military fort, and the Mission San Francisco de Asís, also known as Mission Dolores. These marked the beginning of Spanish settlement in the region. The mission system aimed to convert Native Americans to Christianity and integrate them into the Spanish colonial society.

In 1821, Mexico gained independence from Spain, and San Francisco became part of Mexican territory. During this period, the city was known as Yerba Buena, which means "good herb" in Spanish, a reference to the abundant wild mint growing in the area. The Mexican period saw the expansion of ranchos, large land grants used for cattle farming.

In 1846, during the Mexican-American War, the United States claimed California, and Yerba Buena was soon renamed San Francisco. This change marked the beginning of a significant transformation for the city. Just a few years later, in 1848, gold was discovered at

Sutter's Mill, not far from San Francisco. This discovery sparked the California Gold Rush, one of the most pivotal events in the city's history.

The Gold Rush brought a massive influx of people to San Francisco, transforming it from a small settlement into a booming city almost overnight. Prospectors, entrepreneurs, and adventurers from around the world flocked to the area, seeking fortune and opportunity. The city's population exploded, and it quickly developed into a bustling port and commercial center.

With the rapid growth came the need for infrastructure and services. Streets were laid out, and buildings were constructed at a frenetic pace. San Francisco became known for its lively, often chaotic atmosphere. The city's economy thrived, and it established itself as a major hub for finance, trade, and culture on the West Coast.

In 1906, San Francisco faced one of the most devastating events in its history. A massive earthquake struck the city, followed by a series of fires that raged for several days. Much of the city was destroyed, and thousands of residents were left homeless. Despite this catastrophe, the resilient spirit of the people of San Francisco led to a remarkable recovery. The city was rebuilt, and many of the iconic structures that define San Francisco today were constructed during this period.

The early 20th century saw further growth and development. The completion of major projects like the Golden Gate Bridge and the Bay Bridge connected San

Francisco to surrounding areas and facilitated commerce and travel. The city's diverse population continued to grow, contributing to its rich cultural tapestry.

San Francisco played a significant role during World War II as a major port for the United States Navy. After the war, the city became a center for social and cultural movements. The 1950s and 1960s saw the rise of the Beat Generation and the counterculture movement, with neighborhoods like North Beach and Haight-Ashbury becoming synonymous with artistic and social revolution.

In recent decades, San Francisco has continued to evolve. The technology boom of the late 20th and early 21st centuries brought a new wave of economic prosperity and demographic change. The city became a global center for innovation and technology, attracting talent and investment from around the world.

Today, San Francisco stands as a vibrant, dynamic city with a rich historical legacy. Its history is reflected in its diverse neighborhoods, iconic landmarks, and cultural institutions. Exploring San Francisco is not just about experiencing its present-day attractions but also understanding the historical context that has shaped this unique and fascinating city.

CHAPTER 1

Planning Your Trip

Planning your trip to San Francisco involves several important steps to ensure a smooth and enjoyable experience. This section of the guide provides essential information on the best times to visit, visa requirements, travel insurance, and what to pack. It also covers practical details, like budgeting for your trip. By following these guidelines, you'll be well-prepared to explore San Francisco's diverse attractions and vibrant neighborhoods. This guide will help you make informed decisions and maximise your time in this iconic city.

Deciding When to Visit

Deciding when to visit San Francisco is crucial to enjoying all that this beautiful city has to offer. San Francisco's unique climate and seasonal events can greatly influence your travel experience. Understanding the best times to visit can help you plan an unforgettable trip.

San Francisco experiences a mild Mediterranean climate with cool, wet winters and dry, warm summers. However, the city's coastal location also means it has a unique weather pattern characterised by frequent fog, especially in the summer months. The best time to visit San Francisco, widely considered by travel experts, is during the fall, particularly from September to

November. During these months, the weather is at its warmest and sunniest, with temperatures ranging from 63°F to 70°F during the day. This period, often referred to as San Francisco's "Indian Summer," sees fewer tourists and clearer skies, making it ideal for outdoor activities and sightseeing.

Spring, from March to May, is another excellent time to visit San Francisco. During this season, the city starts to warm up after the winter rains, and the landscape comes alive with blooming flowers and lush greenery. Temperatures are generally pleasant, averaging in the mid-60s °F, and the city experiences less fog compared to the summer months. Spring also offers thinner crowds and lower accommodation rates, making it a favourable time for budget-conscious travellers.

Summer, from June to August, is often cooler and foggier than one might expect. The famous San Francisco fog, known as "Karl the Fog," rolls in from the ocean, particularly in the mornings and evenings, creating a cooler climate with temperatures often staying in the mid-50s to mid-60s °F. Despite the fog, summer is a busy tourist season with numerous festivals and events, such as the Outside Lands Music Festival in August. If you plan to visit during the summer, be prepared for larger crowds and higher prices for flights and accommodations.

Winter, from December to February, is the city's wettest season, with more frequent rainfall and cooler temperatures. Despite this, winter can still be a good time to visit, especially for those looking to avoid crowds. The city is beautifully decorated for the holiday season, and you can enjoy attractions without the usual tourist rush. Temperatures generally remain moderate, rarely dipping below the mid-40s°F, making it manageable with a warm coat and umbrella.

Each season in San Francisco has its own unique charm and offers different experiences. Fall is the best time for warm weather and clear skies, while spring provides blooming landscapes and fewer crowds. Summer brings a lively atmosphere with many events, despite the fog, and winter offers a quieter, more festive experience. By considering these factors, you can choose the best time to visit San Francisco based on your preferences and enjoy everything this vibrant city has to offer.

Climate and Weather

Understanding the climate and weather patterns of San Francisco is crucial for planning your trip. San Francisco is known for its mild Mediterranean climate, characterised by wet winters and dry summers. However, its unique geographic location along the coast significantly influences its weather, creating distinct microclimates throughout the city.

San Francisco's summers are cool and foggy, especially compared to the warmer inland areas of California. From June to August, the city experiences a phenomenon known as "June Gloom," where the mornings are often blanketed in fog that can linger until the afternoon. This fog is caused by the cold ocean waters meeting the warmer inland air, creating a marine layer. Despite the fog, temperatures during the summer generally range from the mid-50s to mid-60s °F (13–18 °C). The afternoons can clear up, offering sunny skies, but it's always a good idea to carry a light jacket.

Autumn, from September to November, is considered the best time to visit San Francisco. During these months, the fog lessens, and the city enjoys its warmest and sunniest weather. Daytime temperatures typically range from the mid-60s to mid-70s °F (18–24 °C), making it ideal for outdoor activities and sightseeing. The reduced fog and comfortable temperatures provide excellent conditions for exploring the city's parks, beaches, and iconic landmarks.

Winter in San Francisco, from December to February, brings cooler and wetter conditions. While the temperatures remain relatively mild, rarely dropping below 45°F (7°C), the city sees increased rainfall. January tends to be the wettest month, with an average of about 4.5 inches (114 mm) of rain. Despite the rain, the winter months can be a good time to visit if you prefer fewer tourists and don't mind occasional showers. It's advisable to pack a raincoat and an umbrella to stay dry during your excursions.

Spring, from March to May, offers a pleasant mix of mild temperatures and blooming landscapes. The city starts to warm up after the winter rains, with daytime temperatures ranging from the mid-50s to mid-60s°F (13–18°C) in March, gradually increasing to the high

60s°F (around 20°C) by May. Springtime also brings fewer tourists compared to the summer, making it a great time to enjoy the city's attractions without the crowds. The blooming flowers and green hills add a touch of beauty to the city's parks and gardens.

San Francisco's unique microclimates can cause significant variations in weather, even within short distances. For example, the Sunset and Richmond districts, located near the ocean, are often cooler and foggier than neighbourhoods like the Mission District and SoMa, which tend to be sunnier and warmer. This variability means it's important to dress in layers, allowing you to adjust to changing conditions throughout the day.

Wind is another characteristic of San Francisco's weather, particularly near the waterfront and on the hills. The cool sea breeze can make the temperatures feel colder than they are, so having a windbreaker can be helpful.

San Francisco's climate is relatively moderate year-round, with no extreme temperatures. Understanding the seasonal patterns and microclimates will help you pack appropriately and plan your activities to make the most of your visit.

Visa Requirements

Understanding visa requirements is essential for planning a smooth trip to San Francisco. Depending on your nationality, the requirements can vary significantly.

San Francisco, like the rest of the United States, has specific entry requirements. Most travellers need a visa to enter the U.S., but some countries participate in the Visa Waiver Programme (VWP), allowing their citizens to visit for up to 90 days without a visa. Countries in the VWP include most of the European Union, Australia, Japan, and South Korea, among others. Travellers from these countries must apply for authorization through the Electronic System for Travel Authorization (ESTA) at least 72 hours before departure. This authorization is valid for two years or until your passport expires, whichever comes first.

For travellers from countries not included in the VWP, obtaining a visa is mandatory. The most common type of visa for tourists is the B-2 visitor visa, which covers tourism, vacation, and visits to friends or relatives. To apply for a B-2 visa, you must complete the DS-160 form online, pay the visa application fee, and schedule an interview at the nearest U.S. embassy or consulate. During the interview, you will need to provide various documents, including a valid passport, a photograph, and evidence of ties to your home country, such as employment, family, or property, to demonstrate your intent to return after your visit.

In addition to the standard documentation, certain travellers might need to provide additional information or meet specific requirements. For example, if you have visited countries considered high-risk for certain communicable diseases, you might need to show proof of vaccination or undergo medical screening. It's crucial

25

to check the latest health advisories and entry requirements before your trip to ensure compliance.

Canadian citizens do not need a visa to enter the United States but must present a valid passport and proof of residence. They can stay in the U.S. for up to six months without a visa. However, they must still comply with all other entry requirements and may be subject to additional checks upon arrival.

For all travellers, it's important to ensure that your passport is valid for at least six months beyond your planned departure date from the United States. This rule applies to most nationalities, although some countries have agreements with the U.S. that waive this requirement. Always verify the specific requirements for your country before travelling.

Applying for a visa or ESTA in advance is crucial, as processing times can vary. While ESTA approvals are often granted within a few hours, it's recommended to apply at least 72 hours before your trip. Visa applications, on the other hand, can take several weeks, especially during peak travel seasons. Planning ahead ensures that you have enough time to gather all the necessary documents and complete the application process without stress.

Understanding and fulfilling the visa requirements is a key step in planning your trip to San Francisco. For the most accurate and up-to-date information, always check the official U.S. Department of State website or contact the nearest U.S. embassy or consulate in your country.

Travel Insurance

Travel insurance is an essential component of planning a trip to San Francisco. It provides a safety net against unforeseen circumstances that could disrupt your travel plans and lead to significant expenses. This part of this guide gives an explanation of why travel insurance is important and what it typically covers.

Medical Emergencies

One of the primary reasons to purchase travel insurance is to cover medical emergencies. Healthcare in San Francisco is known to be expensive, and if you fall ill or have an accident, the costs can quickly add up. Travel insurance can cover expenses such as hospital stays, doctor's fees, and even emergency medical evacuations. This ensures that you receive the necessary treatment without worrying about the financial burden.

Trip Cancellation and Interruption

Travel insurance often includes coverage for trip cancellations or interruptions. If you need to cancel your trip due to illness, family emergencies, or other covered reasons, travel insurance can reimburse you for non-refundable expenses like flights, hotels, and tours. Similarly, if your trip is interrupted for reasons covered by your policy, you can be reimbursed for the unused portion of your trip as well as any additional expenses incurred to return home.

Baggage Loss and Delay

Losing your baggage or having it delayed can be a major inconvenience. Travel insurance can provide compensation for essential items if your luggage is delayed, lost, or stolen. This means you can purchase necessary clothing and toiletries without bearing the extra costs out of pocket.

Travel Delays

San Francisco's weather, particularly its famous fog, can sometimes lead to flight delays. Travel insurance can cover additional expenses incurred due to delays, such as meals and accommodations. This can be particularly useful if you have connecting flights and miss them due to delays.

Emergency Evacuation and Repatriation

In the event of a serious medical emergency, travel insurance can cover the costs of evacuation to the nearest appropriate medical facility or even repatriation to your home country. This coverage is crucial for ensuring you receive the best possible care and can return home safely if needed.

Specialty Coverage

Some travel insurance plans offer additional coverage options, such as "Cancel for Any Reason" insurance, which provides more flexibility to cancel your trip under a broader range of circumstances. This can be particularly beneficial if you are unsure about your travel plans or if unexpected events occur.

Cost of Travel Insurance

The cost of travel insurance typically ranges from 3% to 10% of your total trip cost, depending on factors such as the length of your trip, your age, and the level of coverage you choose. It's a small investment compared to the potential costs of medical emergencies, trip cancellations, or other unexpected events.

Travel insurance provides comprehensive coverage that can protect you from the financial risks associated with traveling. Having insurance ensures peace of mind and allows you to enjoy your trip to San Francisco without worrying about the unexpected. Always read the policy details carefully to understand what is covered and to choose the plan that best meets your needs.

Packing Essentials for San Francisco

Packing for a trip to San Francisco requires a bit of planning due to the city's unique weather patterns and diverse activities. San Francisco is known for its microclimates, meaning the weather can vary significantly from one neighbourhood to another and even within the same day. This part of this guide would help you pack appropriately and ensure a comfortable and enjoyable visit.

Layers, Layers, Layers

The key to dressing in San Francisco is layering. The city's weather can change rapidly, and it's not uncommon to experience fog, wind, and sunshine all in one day. Start with a base layer like a t-shirt or light shirt, add a middle layer such as a sweater or hoodie, and top it off with a light, windproof jacket. This way, you can easily add or remove layers as the temperature fluctuates. Even in the summer, evenings can be chilly, so always carry an extra layer.

Comfortable Walking Shoes

San Francisco is a city best explored on foot, but its famous hills can be challenging. Comfortable, closed-toe walking shoes are essential. Sneakers or hiking shoes are ideal, as they provide the support needed for walking up and down steep streets and navigating uneven sidewalks. Avoid flip-flops or any shoes that might not offer sufficient support or grip.

Rain Gear

Although San Francisco does not experience heavy rainfall year-round, it's wise to be prepared, especially if you are visiting in the winter months. A lightweight, waterproof rain jacket will keep you dry without taking up much space in your bag. Additionally, a compact umbrella can be handy for unexpected showers.

Accessories for Warmth

Accessories like scarves, gloves, and hats can make a big difference in keeping warm, especially in the evenings when temperatures drop. These items are lightweight and easy to carry, making them practical additions to your packing list. A warm hat, in particular, can help protect against the chill and wind.

Day Bag

A good day bag is essential for carrying your daily necessities while exploring the city. Choose a comfortable backpack or crossbody bag that can hold your extra layers, water bottle, camera, and any souvenirs you might pick up along the way. Consider a bag with secure compartments to keep your valuables safe.

Sun Protection

Despite the frequent fog, UV rays can still be strong in San Francisco. Sunscreen, sunglasses, and a hat will help protect you from sunburn, especially when the fog clears and the sun shines through. A reusable water bottle is also useful to stay hydrated during your adventures.

Jeans and versatile clothing

Jeans are a staple in San Francisco's casual style. They are versatile and suitable for most activities and dining experiences in the city. Pair them with various tops and layers to adapt to the changing weather. Comfortable, casual clothing that you can mix and match will serve you well throughout your trip.

Packing Tips for Specific Seasons

-Spring and Fall

These seasons offer mild weather, but it can still be unpredictable. Pack layers and a mix of warm and cool-weather clothing. A light jacket and raincoat are advisable.

-Summer

Even in the summer, San Francisco can be cool, especially in the mornings and evenings. Light layers are key, along with a warm jacket for the cooler parts of the day.

-Winter

Winters are generally cool and wet. In addition to your regular layers, ensure you have a waterproof jacket and warm accessories like hats and gloves to stay comfortable during rainy spells.

By packing thoughtfully and preparing for the varied climate, you'll be well-equipped to enjoy all that San Francisco has to offer.

Budgeting

Creating a budget for your trip to San Francisco is essential for managing your expenses and ensuring a stress-free visit. San Francisco is known for being one of the more expensive cities in the United States, but with careful planning, you can make the most of your trip without overspending.

Accommodation Costs

Accommodation will likely be one of the largest expenses. San Francisco offers a range of options, from luxury hotels to budget-friendly hostels. On average, a mid-range hotel can cost between $150 and $300 per night. If you're looking for a more economical option, consider staying in hostels, which can cost around $30 to $50 per night for a dorm bed. Vacation rentals, such as those found on Airbnb, can also provide cost-effective alternatives, especially for longer stays or larger groups.

Transportation

Getting around San Francisco can be cost-effective if you plan wisely. The city has an extensive public transportation system, including buses, streetcars, and the famous cable cars. A single ride on MUNI (Municipal Transportation Agency) costs around $3, but you can save money with a MUNI Passport, which offers unlimited rides for one, three, or seven days. The Bay Area Rapid Transit (BART) system is useful for trips to and from the airport and surrounding areas, with fares varying based on distance. If you plan to use rideshares or taxis, budget for higher costs, as these can add up quickly, especially during peak times.

Food and Dining

San Francisco is a food lover's paradise, with a wide range of dining options to suit every budget. Budget for around $10 to $15 per meal at casual eateries and food trucks. Mid-range restaurants might cost between $20 and $40 per person, while fine dining establishments can be significantly more expensive. To save money, consider exploring local markets and grocery stores for snacks and meals. The Ferry Building Marketplace offers a variety of gourmet food options and is a great place to enjoy a meal without breaking the bank.

Attractions and Activities

Many of San Francisco's iconic attractions, such as the Golden Gate Bridge, Fisherman's Wharf, and Lombard Street, are free to visit. However, entry fees to museums and other attractions can add up. Budget for around $15 to $30 per person for entry to popular sites like the California Academy of Sciences, the Exploratorium, or Alcatraz Island. Consider purchasing a CityPASS, which offers discounted entry to multiple attractions and can save you money if you plan to visit several paid sites.

Shopping and Souvenirs

If you plan to do some shopping or purchase souvenirs, set aside a portion of your budget for this. San Francisco has diverse shopping options, from high-end boutiques to local artisan markets. Union Square is a popular shopping destination, but be prepared for higher prices.

For unique and affordable souvenirs, visit places like Chinatown or local markets.

Miscellaneous Expenses

Don't forget to budget for miscellaneous expenses such as tips, taxes, and emergency funds. Tipping is customary in the United States, with 15-20% being standard for restaurant service. Sales tax in San Francisco is around 8.5%, which is added to most purchases. It's also wise to have a small emergency fund for unexpected expenses, such as medical needs or travel disruptions.

Sample Daily Budget

Accommodation: $150

Transportation: $10 (public transportation)

Food: $50 (breakfast, lunch, dinner, and snacks)

Attractions: $20 (entry to one paid attraction)

Miscellaneous: $20 (tips, taxes, and other expenses)

Total: $250 per day.

By planning your budget carefully and considering these expenses, you can enjoy all that San Francisco has to offer without financial stress. Remember to track your spending throughout your trip to stay within your budget and make adjustments as needed. This will help ensure a smooth and enjoyable visit to the City by the Bay.

CHAPTER 2

Neighbourhoods

San Francisco is a city renowned for its diverse and distinctive neighbourhoods, each offering a unique atmosphere and experience. Exploring these neighbourhoods provides an understanding of the city's culture, history, and vibrant community life.

Union Square

Scan the QR code to see the map of Union Square

Union Square is the vibrant heart of San Francisco, known for its upscale shopping, diverse dining, and bustling entertainment. This lively district offers a variety of attractions, making it a must-visit destination for tourists.

Attractions

Union Square boasts numerous attractions that cater to all interests. The central plaza, Union Square Park, is surrounded by an array of high-end department stores like Macy's, Neiman Marcus, and Saks Fifth Avenue. Art enthusiasts can visit the Martin Lawrence Galleries, while theatre lovers can catch a show at the San Francisco Playhouse. Seasonal events such as the Holiday Ice Rink in Union Square add to the charm of this bustling district.

Getting There From Major Airports

San Francisco International Airport (SFO) is the main gateway to the city, located about 12 miles from Union Square. The most efficient way to reach Union Square from SFO is by taking the BART (Bay Area Rapid Transit) to Powell Street Station, which is a short walk from the square. This journey takes about 30 minutes. From Oakland International Airport (OAK), you can also take the BART, transferring at the Coliseum Station to reach Powell Street in about 50 minutes. If flying into Norman Y. Mineta San Jose International Airport (SJC), the trip involves taking the Caltrain from Santa Clara

Station to San Francisco, followed by a short bus or taxi ride.

Accommodation Options

Union Square offers a range of accommodation options to suit different budgets and preferences. For luxury stays, consider The Westin St. Francis or Hotel Nikko San Francisco. Mid-range travellers might opt for Hotel Abri or the Handlery Union Square Hotel, while budget-conscious visitors can find quality stays at the HI San Francisco Downtown Hostel.

Transportation Options

Getting around Union Square is convenient, with various transportation options. Public transit, including BART and MUNI buses and streetcars, provides extensive coverage. Taxis and rideshares like Uber and Lyft are readily available. The area is also highly walkable, allowing visitors to explore many attractions on foot.

Recommended Restaurants

Union Square's dining scene caters to all tastes. Solo travellers can enjoy a sophisticated meal at The Rotunda at Neiman Marcus. Couples might prefer the romantic ambiance of Farallon for a seafood dinner. Families will appreciate the diverse menu at The Cheesecake Factory, while groups can head to Scala's Bistro for a lively dining experience. Other notable mentions include Tacorea for Mexican cuisine, Bouche for French delicacies, and Honey Honey Cafe & Crepery for a casual bite.

For solo travellers, Union Square's walkability and plethora of cafes and galleries make it an ideal place to explore independently. Couples can enjoy the area's intimate dining options and theatre performances. Families will find the seasonal events and central location convenient for sightseeing. Groups can take advantage of the vibrant nightlife and spacious restaurants.

When visiting Union Square, avoid visiting late at night, when the area can become deserted. Be cautious of street vendors offering items without clear prices, as overcharging can occur. Watch out for scams involving "free" gifts that require donations, and stick to recognised transportation options to ensure safety.

Chinatown

Scan the QR code to see the map of Chinatown

Chinatown, in San Francisco, is one of the oldest and most established Chinese communities outside of Asia. It offers a rich cultural experience with its vibrant streets, historical landmarks, and unique shops. Entering through the iconic Dragon Gate on Grant Avenue, visitors are greeted with colourful shops, traditional Chinese architecture, and a bustling atmosphere.

40

Attractions

Chinatown is filled with attractions that reflect its cultural heritage and vibrant community. The Chinese Historical Society of America Museum provides insight into the history and contributions of Chinese Americans. Portsmouth Square, often referred to as the "heart of Chinatown," is a lively park where locals practice Tai Chi, play chess, and socialize. Other notable attractions include the Tin How Temple, one of the oldest Chinese temples in the United States, and the Golden Gate Fortune Cookie Factory, where visitors can see how fortune cookies are made and even create their own custom messages.

Getting There From Major Airports

From San Francisco International Airport (SFO), Chinatown is accessible by taking the BART (Bay Area Rapid Transit) to Montgomery Street Station, followed by a short walk. The total journey takes about 40 minutes. From Oakland International Airport (OAK), the BART ride involves a transfer at the Coliseum Station to reach Montgomery Street in approximately 50 minutes. From Norman Y. Mineta San Jose International Airport (SJC), the trip involves taking the Caltrain to San Francisco, then a short bus or taxi ride to Chinatown.

Accommodation Options

Chinatown offers a range of accommodation options. For luxury stays, the nearby Ritz-Carlton provides upscale amenities. Mid-range options include the Hilton San

Francisco Financial District, which offers comfortable accommodations with convenient access to Chinatown. Budget travellers can consider the San Francisco Inn, which provides basic amenities at affordable rates.

Transportation Options

Navigating Chinatown is easy, with several transportation options. The area is highly walkable, allowing visitors to explore its many attractions on foot. Public transit, including MUNI buses and streetcars, provides extensive coverage. Taxis and rideshares like Uber and Lyft are also readily available for convenient travel.

Recommended Restaurants

Chinatown is a food lover's paradise with a wide variety of dining options. Solo travellers can enjoy a meal at Z & Y Restaurant, known for its authentic Szechuan cuisine. Couples might prefer the intimate setting of China Live, which offers a modern twist on classic Chinese dishes. Families will appreciate the extensive menu at R&G Lounge, famous for its salt and pepper crab. Groups can enjoy a communal dining experience at Great Eastern Restaurant, where dim sum is highly recommended.

Chinatown's vibrant streets and cultural richness make it an ideal destination for all types of travelers. Solo travellers will find plenty of cafes and small shops to explore. Couples can enjoy romantic walks through the picturesque alleys and visits to tea houses. Families will find the area's cultural attractions and parks entertaining and educational. Groups can take advantage of the numerous dining options and guided tours.

Chinatown offers a unique and immersive experience, blending historical significance with modern vibrancy. Its attractions, dining, and cultural offerings make it a must-visit district in San Francisco, ensuring every visitor leaves with memorable experiences.

North Beach

Scan the QR code to see the map of North Beach

North Beach, often referred to as San Francisco's Little Italy, is a vibrant district known for its rich cultural history, delicious cuisine, and lively nightlife. It is a place where the charm of old-world Italy meets the dynamic energy of San Francisco, offering visitors an unforgettable experience.

Attractions

North Beach is packed with attractions that reflect its cultural heritage and bohemian past. One must-visit spot is the historic City Lights Bookstore, a literary landmark that played a pivotal role in the Beat Generation. The Beat Museum, just a short walk away, offers deeper insights into this influential movement. Washington Square Park is the heart of North Beach, a perfect spot to relax and watch locals play bocce ball. Saints Peter and Paul Church, located on the north side of the park, is another iconic site, famous for its stunning architecture and historical significance.

Getting There From Major Airports

From San Francisco International Airport (SFO), North Beach can be reached by taking the BART (Bay Area Rapid Transit) to Montgomery Street Station, followed by a short MUNI bus ride or a 15-minute walk. This journey takes about 45 minutes. From Oakland International Airport (OAK), take the BART to Embarcadero Station and then a MUNI bus or streetcar to North Beach, taking around 50 minutes in total. From Norman Y. Mineta San Jose International Airport (SJC), the trip involves taking the Caltrain to San Francisco, then a bus or taxi to North Beach, totaling approximately 1.5 hours.

Accommodation Options

North Beach offers a variety of accommodations to suit different budgets. For luxury, the Fairmont Heritage Place Ghirardelli Square offers upscale amenities with beautiful views of the bay. Mid-range travellers can stay at Hotel Boheme, which captures the artistic spirit of the neighbourhood. Budget options include the Green Tortoise Hostel, known for its friendly atmosphere and excellent location.

Transportation Options

Exploring North Beach is easy and convenient. The neighbourhood is very walkable, allowing you to enjoy its narrow streets and hidden gems on foot. MUNI buses and streetcars provide extensive coverage for those who prefer public transit. Taxis and rideshares like Uber and Lyft are readily available for quick trips around the city.

Recommended Restaurants

North Beach is a food lover's paradise with a wide range of dining options. Solo travellers can enjoy a cosy meal at the famous Caffe Trieste, a historic cafe known for its excellent coffee and vibrant atmosphere. Couples might opt for a romantic dinner at Sotto Mare Oysteria & Seafood, renowned for its fresh seafood and intimate setting. Families will appreciate Tony's Pizza Napoletana, offering a variety of pizzas that are sure to please everyone. Groups can head to Original Joe's for a lively dining experience with classic Italian-American dishes.

North Beach captures the essence of San Francisco with its blend of cultural history, culinary delights, and vibrant nightlife. Its attractions, dining options, and friendly atmosphere make it a must-visit district in the city, ensuring every visitor has a memorable experience.

Financial District

Scan the QR code to see the map of Financial District

The Financial District in San Francisco is the bustling business hub of the city, filled with towering skyscrapers, historic landmarks, and a dynamic blend of commerce and culture. It's home to some of the most iconic buildings and offers a range of activities and amenities for visitors.

Attractions

The Financial District boasts several notable attractions. The Transamerica Pyramid is a standout architectural marvel, symbolising the city's skyline. The Wells Fargo History Museum offers insights into the Gold Rush era and banking history. Pier 24 Photography Museum, a hidden gem, showcases contemporary photography with curated exhibits. Transamerica Redwood Park provides a serene escape with its beautiful trees and sculptures. Historic sites like the Flatiron Building and the Federal Reserve Bank Building add to the district's rich heritage.

Getting There From Major Airports

From San Francisco International Airport (SFO), take the BART to Montgomery Street Station, a journey of about 30 minutes. From Oakland International Airport (OAK), take the BART with a transfer at the Coliseum Station, reaching Montgomery Street Station in approximately 45 minutes. From Norman Y. Mineta San Jose International Airport (SJC), the trip involves taking the Caltrain to San Francisco, followed by a short bus or taxi ride, totaling about 1.5 hours.

Accommodation Options

The Financial District offers a range of accommodations. Luxury seekers can stay at the Omni San Francisco Hotel or the Ritz-Carlton, both of which offer premium amenities and services. Mid-range options like the Hilton San Francisco Financial District provide comfort and convenience. Budget travellers can find more affordable options nearby in areas like Union Square.

Transportation Options

Navigating the Financial District is easy with extensive transportation options. The area is very walkable, allowing visitors to explore it on foot. Public transit, including BART and MUNI buses, provides excellent coverage. Taxis and rideshares like Uber and Lyft are readily available for quick trips around the city.

Recommended Restaurants

Dining in the Financial District offers something for everyone. Solo travellers can enjoy a quick and delicious meal at Tadich Grill, one of the oldest restaurants in California. Couples might prefer the romantic ambiance of Kokkari Estiatorio, known for its Mediterranean cuisine. Families will appreciate the diverse menu at Wayfare Tavern, offering American comfort food in a family-friendly setting. Groups can enjoy the lively atmosphere and shared plates at Perbacco, specialising in Italian cuisine.

Solo travellers can explore the district's many cafes and historic sites at their own pace. Couples can enjoy romantic dinners and scenic walks through Redwood Park. Families will find the district's museums and open spaces welcoming. Groups can take advantage of the district's vibrant nightlife and extensive dining options.

The Financial District provides a unique and engaging experience for all visitors.

Nob Hill

Scan the QR code to see the map of Nob Hill

Nob Hill, a swanky and stylish neighbourhood in San Francisco, is renowned for its rich history, breathtaking architecture, and stunning views. This area, once home to the city's most affluent residents, now attracts visitors with its elegant landmarks and cultural attractions.

Attractions

Nob Hill is packed with significant landmarks and attractions. Grace Cathedral, with its Gothic architecture and beautiful labyrinths, is a serene spot for contemplation and admiration. Nearby, the Cable Car Museum offers an intriguing look at San Francisco's iconic cable car system. The historic streetcars add a nostalgic touch to the neighbourhood, providing both transportation and a unique sightseeing experience. The Fairmont Hotel and the InterContinental Mark Hopkins Hotel are architectural gems offering panoramic views from their respective rooftop lounges, especially the Top of the Mark at the Mark Hopkins.

Getting There From Major Airports

From San Francisco International Airport (SFO), you can reach Nob Hill by taking the BART to Powell Street Station, followed by a short cable car ride or a walk. This journey typically takes about 40 minutes. From Oakland International Airport (OAK), take the BART to Embarcadero Station, then switch to a MUNI bus or cable car. This trip also takes around 50 minutes. From Norman Y. Mineta San Jose International Airport (SJC), the journey involves taking the Caltrain to San

Francisco, then a taxi or bus, taking approximately 1.5 hours.

Accommodation Options

Nob Hill offers a variety of accommodations catering to different tastes and budgets. Luxury options include the Fairmont San Francisco and the InterContinental Mark Hopkins, both offering luxurious amenities and spectacular views. For mid-range stays, consider the Stanford Court Hotel, which blends historic charm with modern comforts. Budget travellers can find affordable options in nearby areas, ensuring a comfortable stay within easy reach of Nob Hill's attractions.

Transportation Options

Exploring Nob Hill is convenient thanks to its walkable nature and various transportation options. The iconic cable cars provide a scenic and historic way to navigate the steep hills. MUNI buses also serve the area, offering extensive coverage throughout San Francisco. Taxis and rideshares like Uber and Lyft are readily available for those preferring quicker transit.

Recommended Restaurants

Dining in Nob Hill caters to a variety of preferences. Solo travellers can enjoy a peaceful meal at the Nob Hill Cafe, known for its cosy atmosphere and delicious Italian cuisine. Couples might opt for a romantic dinner at the Liholiho Yacht Club, which offers a unique blend of Asian and Hawaiian dishes. Families will appreciate the diverse menu at the Big 4 Restaurant, located within the Huntington Hotel, offering a warm and family-friendly setting. Groups can enjoy the lively ambiance at Top of the Mark, perfect for shared plates and cocktails with a view.

Nob Hill encapsulates the elegance and historical richness of San Francisco.

Russian Hill

Scan the QR code to see the map of Russian Hill

Russian Hill is a chic and historic neighbourhood in San Francisco, known for its stunning views, winding streets, and charming atmosphere. It's a place where you can explore iconic landmarks, dine at top-notch restaurants, and enjoy the unique blend of residential tranquilly and vibrant urban life.

Attractions

Russian Hill is home to some of San Francisco's most famous attractions. Lombard Street, often dubbed the "crookedest street in the world," is a must-see with its tight hairpin turns and beautifully landscaped gardens. The San Francisco Art Institute offers not only incredible art exhibits but also a Diego Rivera mural that is a significant piece of art history. Macondray Lane, a hidden gem, provides a peaceful walkway lined with lush gardens and scenic views, famously depicted in Armistead Maupin's "Tales of the City." For a relaxing break, visit Ina Coolbrith Park, which offers one of the best panoramic views of the city.

Getting There From Major Airports

From San Francisco International Airport (SFO), you can reach Russian Hill by taking the BART to Powell Street Station, then transferring to a MUNI bus or enjoying a scenic cable car ride up the hill. This journey takes about 40 minutes. From Oakland International Airport (OAK), take the BART to Embarcadero Station and then switch to a MUNI bus, taking around 50 minutes. If you're coming from Norman Y. Mineta San Jose International Airport (SJC), the trip involves taking the Caltrain to San Francisco, followed by a bus or taxi ride, which takes approximately 1.5 hours.

Accommodation Options

Russian Hill offers a range of accommodations that cater to different preferences and budgets. For luxury stays, consider the Fairmont Heritage Place Ghirardelli Square, which provides upscale amenities and stunning bay views. Mid-range travellers might opt for the Nob Hill Motor Inn, offering comfortable accommodations with easy access to the attractions of Russian Hill. Budget options can be found in nearby neighbourhoods, ensuring a comfortable stay while being close to Russian Hill's highlights.

Transportation Options

Exploring Russian Hill is convenient thanks to its walkable nature and several transportation options. The iconic cable cars provide a scenic and historic way to navigate the steep hills. MUNI buses also serve the area well, offering extensive coverage throughout San Francisco. Taxis and rideshares like Uber and Lyft are readily available for quick and convenient travel.

Recommended Restaurants

Russian Hill boasts a diverse dining scene with options for all types of travelers. Solo travellers can enjoy a meal at Za Pizza, a cosy spot known for its delicious Italian dishes. Couples might prefer the intimate setting of Frascati, offering Mediterranean-inspired cuisine in a romantic ambiance. Families will find a welcoming environment and a diverse menu at Seven Hills, making it perfect for a family dinner. Groups can head to Gary

Danko, a renowned restaurant offering gourmet American cuisine with an extensive wine list, perfect for celebrating special occasions.

Visitors should avoid driving through the narrow, steep streets unless absolutely necessary to avoid traffic and parking difficulties. Stick to recognised transportation options and well-reviewed businesses to ensure a safe and enjoyable visit.

Fisherman's Wharf

Scan the QR code to see the map of Fisherman's Wharf

Fisherman's Wharf is one of San Francisco's most iconic and lively neighbourhoods, known for its waterfront attractions, seafood restaurants, and bustling activity. This historic area offers something for everyone, making it a must-visit destination.

Attractions

Fisherman's Wharf is packed with attractions that cater to a wide range of interests. The famous Pier 39 is a lively spot featuring shops, restaurants, and playful sea lions basking on the docks. The San Francisco Maritime National Historical Park and the Maritime Museum provide fascinating insights into the city's seafaring history. Ghirardelli Square offers not only delicious chocolate but also boutique shopping and stunning views of the bay. The Musee Mecanique is a delightful museum showcasing antique arcade games and mechanical instruments. For panoramic city views, take a ride on the historic cable cars that connect Fisherman's Wharf with other parts of the city.

Getting There From Major Airports

From San Francisco International Airport (SFO), you can reach Fisherman's Wharf by taking the BART to Embarcadero Station, then transferring to a MUNI F-Line streetcar or a bus. This journey typically takes about 50 minutes. From Oakland International Airport (OAK), take the BART to Embarcadero Station and then switch to the MUNI F-Line streetcar, totaling around an hour. From Norman Y. Mineta San Jose International Airport (SJC), the trip involves taking the Caltrain to

San Francisco, then a bus or taxi, taking approximately 1.5 to 2 hours.

Accommodation Options

Fisherman's Wharf offers a variety of accommodations to suit different budgets. Luxury seekers might enjoy a stay at the Argonaut Hotel, which combines historic charm with modern amenities. Mid-range options include the Hotel Zephyr, known for its nautical-themed decor and convenient location. Budget travellers can find comfort and value at the HI San Francisco Fisherman's Wharf Hostel, which offers stunning views and a friendly atmosphere.

Transportation Options

Navigating Fisherman's Wharf is easy thanks to its walkable nature and extensive transportation options. The historic cable cars and MUNI F-Line streetcars provide scenic and convenient access to and from the area. Taxis and rideshares like Uber and Lyft are readily available for quick trips around the city.

Recommended Restaurants

Dining at Fisherman's Wharf is a culinary delight with numerous options to satisfy any palate. Solo travellers can enjoy a meal at the casual Boudin Bakery & Cafe, famous for its clam chowder in a sourdough bread bowl. Couples might prefer the romantic setting of Scoma's, known for its fresh seafood and waterfront views. Families will appreciate the lively atmosphere and extensive menu at The Crab House, perfect for a family dinner. Groups can head to Alioto's for a traditional Italian seafood feast with plenty of room for everyone.

Visitors should be cautious of unsolicited offers for boat tours or other services, as these can sometimes be scams. Stick to recognised transportation options and reputable businesses to ensure a safe and enjoyable visit.

Marina District

Scan the QR code to see the map of Marina District

The Marina District in San Francisco is a picturesque neighbourhood known for its beautiful homes, waterfront views, and vibrant lifestyle. This area, originally developed for the Panama-Pacific International Exposition in 1915, offers a blend of historical significance and modern-day charm, making it a popular destination for both locals and visitors.

Attractions

The Marina District is home to several must-see attractions. The Palace of Fine Arts is an architectural gem with its majestic rotunda and tranquil lagoon, perfect for leisurely strolls and photography. Crissy Field offers stunning views of the Golden Gate Bridge and is ideal for jogging, picnicking, and watching the sunset. The Marina Green provides a spacious area for outdoor activities with panoramic views of the bay. Fort Mason Centre is another highlight, housing art galleries, theatres, and hosting various cultural events throughout the year. For a more laid-back experience, visitors can enjoy the scenic Golden Gate Promenade, which stretches along the waterfront.

Getting There From Major Airports

From San Francisco International Airport (SFO), you can reach the Marina District by taking the BART to Embarcadero Station, then transferring to a MUNI bus or a rideshare. This journey typically takes around 50 minutes. From Oakland International Airport (OAK), take the BART to Embarcadero Station and switch to a MUNI bus, taking approximately an hour. From Norman

Y. Mineta San Jose International Airport (SJC), the trip involves taking the Caltrain to San Francisco, followed by a bus or taxi, totaling about 1.5 to 2 hours.

Accommodation Options

The Marina District offers a variety of accommodations to suit different budgets. Luxury seekers might enjoy staying at the Hotel Del Sol, which offers boutique charm and modern amenities. For mid-range options, consider the Coventry Motor Inn, which provides comfort and convenience close to major attractions. Budget travellers can find value at the nearby HI San Francisco Fisherman's Wharf Hostel, which offers affordable rates and stunning views.

Transportation Options

Navigating the Marina District is easy due to its walkable nature and excellent transportation options. The area is well served by MUNI buses, providing convenient access to other parts of San Francisco. Taxis and rideshares like Uber and Lyft are also readily available, making it easy to get around.

Recommended Restaurants

Dining in the Marina District caters to a variety of tastes and preferences. Solo travellers can enjoy a casual meal at Super Duper Burgers, known for its fresh, fast-food-style offerings. Couples might prefer the romantic ambiance of Atelier Crenn, which offers innovative French cuisine. Families will appreciate the welcoming environment and diverse menu at Pacific Catch, perfect for a family dinner. Groups can head to Delarosa for its lively atmosphere and delicious Italian dishes, making it a great spot for shared meals.

The Marina District is a perfect blend of natural beauty, historical significance, and vibrant urban life, making it a must-visit for anyone travelling to San Francisco.

Pacific Heights

Scan the QR code to see the map of Pacific Heights

Pacific Heights is a prestigious and picturesque neighbourhood in San Francisco, renowned for its stunning views, grand mansions, and serene parks. This area offers a blend of historical elegance and modern-day charm, making it a must-visit for anyone exploring the city.

Attractions

Pacific Heights is home to several notable attractions that showcase its historical and cultural richness. Mrs. Doubtfire House, famous from the beloved film, is a popular spot for photos. The Haas-Lilienthal House, a preserved Victorian mansion, offers guided tours that provide a glimpse into San Francisco's past. Lafayette Park and Alta Plaza Park offer beautiful green spaces with panoramic views of the city and the bay, perfect for a relaxing day out. For a touch of spirituality and history, St. Dominic Church and Congregation Sherith Israel are stunning architectural sites worth visiting.

Getting There From Major Airports

From San Francisco International Airport (SFO), you can reach Pacific Heights by taking the BART to Civic Centre Station, followed by a short taxi or rideshare ride. This journey typically takes about 45 minutes. From Oakland International Airport (OAK), take the BART to Embarcadero Station and then a MUNI bus, taking approximately an hour. From Norman Y. Mineta San Jose International Airport (SJC), the trip involves taking the Caltrain to San Francisco, then a bus or taxi, totaling about 1.5 to 2 hours.

Accommodation Options

Pacific Heights offers a variety of accommodations that cater to different tastes and budgets. For luxury stays, the Hotel Drisco provides upscale amenities and stunning views of the city. Mid-range travellers might enjoy the comfort and convenience of the Jackson Court Hotel, which blends historic charm with modern facilities. Budget travellers can find affordable options in nearby neighbourhoods, ensuring a comfortable stay while being close to Pacific Heights' highlights.

Transportation Options

Navigating Pacific Heights is convenient due to its walkable nature and excellent transportation options. MUNI buses serve the area well, providing access to other parts of San Francisco. Taxis and rideshares like Uber and Lyft are also readily available, making it easy to get around. The neighbourhood's hilly terrain can be challenging, so using public transport for longer distances is advisable.

Recommended Restaurants

Pacific Heights boasts a diverse dining scene with options to suit various preferences. Solo travellers can enjoy a casual meal at **Roam Artisan Burgers**, known for its gourmet burgers. Couples might prefer the intimate setting of SPQR, which offers contemporary Italian cuisine. Families will appreciate the welcoming environment and seafood dishes at Woodhouse Fish Co. Groups can head to The Progress for a communal dining experience with innovative American dishes.

Haight-Ashbury

Scan the QR code to see the map of Haight-Ashbury

Haight-Ashbury is an iconic neighbourhood in San Francisco, famously known as the epicentre of the 1960s counterculture movement. Today, it retains much of its bohemian charm, offering a mix of vintage shops, eclectic eateries, and historic landmarks that make it a vibrant and fascinating area to explore.

Attractions

The heart of Haight-Ashbury is at the intersection of Haight and Ashbury streets, where the spirit of the 1960s is still palpable. Key attractions include the Grateful Dead House and the Jimi Hendrix House, both of which offer glimpses into the lives of legendary musicians who once called this area home. The Jerry Garcia Mural and the Haight-Ashbury Clock are other notable landmarks that celebrate the neighbourhood's rich cultural history. For those interested in quirky sights, the Huge Legs Hanging Out the Window installation is a must-see.

The Psychedelic SF Gallery showcases art inspired by the neighbourhood's storied past, while Amoeba Music is a haven for music lovers with its vast collection of records and CDs. Buena Vista Park offers a serene escape with trails leading to panoramic city views, perfect for a leisurely stroll or meditation.

Getting There From Major Airports

From San Francisco International Airport (SFO), you can reach Haight-Ashbury by taking the BART to Civic Centre Station, then transferring to a MUNI bus. This journey typically takes about 50 minutes. From Oakland International Airport (OAK), take the BART to 16th Street Mission Station and switch to a MUNI bus, totaling around an hour. From Norman Y. Mineta San Jose International Airport (SJC), the trip involves taking the Caltrain to San Francisco, followed by a bus or taxi ride, which takes approximately 1.5 to 2 hours.

Accommodation Options

Haight-Ashbury offers a variety of accommodations. For a boutique experience, the Metro Hotel provides stylish rooms and personalised service. Mid-range options include the Stanyan Park Hotel, offering Victorian charm and modern comforts. Budget travellers can find affordable stays at the nearby Green Tortoise Hostel, which offers a friendly atmosphere and communal facilities.

Transportation Options

Navigating Haight-Ashbury is easy with its walkable streets and excellent public transportation options. MUNI buses serve the area well, providing convenient access to other parts of San Francisco. Taxis and rideshares like Uber and Lyft are also readily available, making it easy to get around.

Recommended Restaurants

Dining in Haight-Ashbury caters to a variety of tastes. Solo travellers can enjoy a casual meal at Pork Store Cafe, known for its hearty breakfasts and friendly vibe. Couples might prefer the intimate setting of Magnolia Pub & Brewery, offering craft beers and delicious American fare. Families will appreciate the diverse menu at Cha Cha Cha, which serves flavorful Latin dishes in a lively environment. Groups can head to Zazie, a French bistro that's perfect for a shared dining experience.

Castro

Scan the QR code to see the map of Castro

The Castro District in San Francisco is a vibrant, historic neighbourhood that has played a pivotal role in the LGBTQ+ rights movement. Known for its colourful streets, rich cultural heritage, and lively atmosphere, the Castro is a must-visit for anyone exploring the city.

Attractions

The Castro is home to several iconic attractions. The Castro Theatre is a beloved landmark with its stunning architecture and classic film screenings. The GLBT

Historical Society Museum offers an in-depth look at the history and culture of the LGBTQ+ community. Harvey Milk Plaza, named after the pioneering gay rights activist, is another significant site, featuring the Rainbow Flag and memorials celebrating LGBTQ+ history. Visitors can also explore Pink Triangle Park, a small but poignant memorial to the LGBTQ+ victims of the Holocaust.

For those interested in shopping and unique finds, Cliff's Variety offers an eclectic mix of goods, and Spark Arts showcases local art. The Twin Peaks Tavern and Badlands are popular nightlife spots known for their welcoming atmosphere and lively crowds.

Getting There From Major Airports

From San Francisco International Airport (SFO), the Castro can be reached by taking the BART to Civic Centre Station, then transferring to a MUNI bus or streetcar. This journey typically takes about 45 minutes. From Oakland International Airport (OAK), take the BART to Embarcadero Station and then a MUNI bus or streetcar, taking approximately 50 minutes. From Norman Y. Mineta San Jose International Airport (SJC), the trip involves taking the Caltrain to San Francisco, followed by a bus or taxi, totaling about 1.5 to 2 hours.

Accommodation Options

The Castro offers a variety of accommodations. For a boutique experience, consider The Hotel Castro, which provides modern amenities and personalised service.

Mid-range travellers might enjoy the comfort of the Beck's Motor Lodge, known for its convenience and friendly atmosphere. Budget travellers can find affordable stays at the nearby Perramont Hotel, which offers basic amenities at a lower cost.

Transportation Options

Navigating the Castro is easy with its walkable streets and excellent public transportation. The MUNI F-Line streetcars provide scenic and convenient access to other parts of San Francisco. Taxis and rideshares like Uber and Lyft are also readily available, making it easy to get around.

Recommended Restaurants

Dining in the Castro caters to a variety of tastes. Solo travellers can enjoy a casual meal at Harvey's, known for its hearty American fare and vibrant atmosphere. Couples might prefer the intimate setting of Frances, which offers upscale French cuisine. Families will appreciate the diverse menu at Starbelly, which is perfect for a family-friendly dining experience. Groups can head to The Sausage Factory, an Italian restaurant with a lively ambiance and ample seating for larger parties.

Mission District

Scan the QR code to see the map of Mission District

The Mission District, often simply referred to as "The Mission," is one of San Francisco's most vibrant and culturally rich neighborhoods. Known for its colourful murals, historic sites, and diverse culinary scene, this area offers a unique blend of Latino heritage and contemporary urban culture.

Attractions

The Mission District is renowned for its stunning street art, with murals adorning buildings and alleyways throughout the neighborhood. Balmy Alley and Clarion Alley are must-visit spots, showcasing a variety of murals that reflect social, political, and cultural themes. Mission Dolores Park is a popular gathering spot for locals and visitors alike, offering beautiful city views, green spaces for picnicking, and recreational activities. The historic Mission San Francisco de Asís (also known as Mission Dolores) is the oldest surviving structure in San Francisco, providing a fascinating glimpse into the city's past. For a dose of local theatre, The Marsh and Victoria Theatre offer a range of performances, from comedy to drama.

Getting There From Major Airports

From San Francisco International Airport (SFO), you can reach the Mission District by taking the BART to the 16th Street Mission Station, a journey that takes about 30 minutes. From Oakland International Airport (OAK), take the BART to the 16th Street Mission Station, with a transfer at the Coliseum Station, totaling approximately 45 minutes. From Norman Y. Mineta San Jose International Airport (SJC), the trip involves taking the Caltrain to San Francisco and then a short bus or taxi ride, which takes about 1.5 to 2 hours.

Accommodation Options

The Mission District offers a range of accommodations. For a boutique experience, consider the Inn San Francisco, which provides a charming bed-and-breakfast experience with Victorian decor. Mid-range travellers might enjoy the Parker Guest House, which offers comfortable rooms and a welcoming atmosphere. Budget travellers can find affordable options at nearby hostels and budget hotels, ensuring a comfortable stay close to the heart of the mission.

Transportation Options

Navigating the Mission District is convenient, with several transportation options. The neighbourhood is very walkable, allowing visitors to explore its many attractions on foot. MUNI buses and BART provide extensive coverage, making it easy to reach other parts of San Francisco. Taxis and rideshares like Uber and Lyft are also readily available for quick trips around the city.

Recommended Restaurants

Dining in the Mission District caters to a variety of tastes. Solo travellers can enjoy a casual meal at La Taqueria, famous for its delicious burritos and tacos. Couples might prefer the romantic ambiance of Foreign Cinema, which offers Californian cuisine and outdoor film screenings. Families will appreciate the diverse menu at Gracias Madre, serving organic, vegan Mexican food in a family-friendly setting. Groups can head to Loló, known for its vibrant decor and inventive Mexican dishes, perfect for shared dining experiences.

South of Market (SoMa)

Scan the QR code to see the map of South of Market

South of Market, commonly known as SoMa, is a dynamic and expansive district in San Francisco known for its blend of industrial charm and modern sophistication. This area, once filled with warehouses, has transformed into a hub of art, culture, and innovation, making it a vibrant place to explore.

Attractions

SoMa is rich with attractions that cater to a variety of interests. The San Francisco Museum of Modern Art

(SFMOMA) is a world-renowned museum featuring an impressive collection of contemporary and modern art. Just a short walk away, Yerba Buena Gardens offers a peaceful retreat with beautiful landscapes, public art, and cultural events. The Contemporary Jewish Museum and the Museum of the African Diaspora provide deep dives into cultural histories and contemporary issues.

For those interested in tech and innovation, the Salesforce Park atop the Salesforce Transit Centre offers a unique elevated green space with stunning city views and frequent public events. Oracle Park, home to the San Francisco Giants, is a must-visit for baseball fans, offering stunning views of the bay. The Children's Creativity Museum is perfect for families, providing interactive exhibits and creative activities for kids.

Getting There From Major Airports

From San Francisco International Airport (SFO), you can reach SoMa by taking the BART to Montgomery Street Station, then transferring to a MUNI bus or walking a short distance. This journey typically takes about 40 minutes. From Oakland International Airport (OAK), take the BART to Embarcadero Station and then a MUNI bus, taking around 50 minutes. From Norman Y. Mineta San Jose International Airport (SJC), the trip involves taking the Caltrain to San Francisco, followed by a bus or taxi, totaling about 1.5 to 2 hours.

Accommodation Options

SoMa offers a variety of accommodations suitable for different budgets and preferences. Luxury travellers might enjoy staying at the St. Regis San Francisco, known for its upscale amenities and prime location. Mid-range options include the Hotel Zetta San Francisco, which combines modern style with comfort. Budget-conscious travellers can find affordable stays at nearby hostels or budget hotels like the HI San Francisco Downtown Hostel.

Transportation Options

Navigating SoMa is convenient with its excellent public transportation options. The area is well served by MUNI buses and light rail, providing easy access to other parts of San Francisco. The neighbourhood's walkability also makes it easy to explore on foot. Taxis and rideshares like Uber and Lyft are readily available for quick and convenient travel.

Recommended Restaurants

Dining in SoMa is a delight with its diverse culinary scene. Solo travellers can enjoy a casual meal at Rooster & Rice, known for its delicious and healthy chicken rice bowls. Couples might prefer the intimate setting of Roku for a modern Japanese dining experience. Families will appreciate the welcoming environment and diverse menu at The American Grilled Cheese Kitchen, perfect for a family-friendly dining experience. Groups can head to Fogo de Chão, a Brazilian steakhouse offering a lively atmosphere and a wide variety of meats and sides.

Tenderloin

Scan the QR code to see the map of Tenderloin

The Tenderloin is a gritty and diverse neighbourhood in San Francisco, known for its rich history, vibrant arts scene, and social activism. While it has a reputation for being a bit rough around the edges, it offers a unique glimpse into the city's multifaceted character.

Attractions

The tenderloin boasts several intriguing attractions. The Tenderloin Museum provides an insightful look into the neighbourhood's storied past and its role in social movements, particularly LGBTQ+ rights. It offers exhibits, photographs, and even walking tours that highlight significant historical sites. Aunt Charlie's Lounge, one of the last remaining gay bars from the 1960s, offers an authentic dive bar experience and drag shows. The Hibernia Bank building, with its stunning architecture, adds a touch of historical grandeur to the area.

Boeddeker Park serves as a community hub with its playground, gardens, and regular events. The Golden Gate Theatre is a beautiful venue that hosts Broadway shows and other performances, providing a cultural counterpoint to the district's street-level grittiness.

Getting There From Major Airports

From San Francisco International Airport (SFO), you can reach the tenderloin by taking the BART to Powell Street Station, followed by a short walk. This journey typically takes about 40 minutes. From Oakland International Airport (OAK), take the BART to 16th Street Mission Station and then a MUNI bus, taking approximately 45 minutes. From Norman Y. Mineta San Jose International Airport (SJC), the trip involves taking the Caltrain to San Francisco, then a bus or taxi, totaling about 1.5 to 2 hours.

Accommodation Options

The Tenderloin offers a range of accommodations that are generally more budget-friendly compared to other parts of San Francisco. For a boutique experience, consider the Phoenix Hotel, which offers a unique, rock-n-roll vibe and a lively atmosphere. Mid-range travellers might enjoy the Hotel Bijou, known for its thematic décor inspired by classic cinema. Budget travellers can find affordable stays at places like the Adrian Hotel, which offers basic amenities at lower costs.

Transportation Options

Navigating the Tenderloin is straightforward, with several transportation options. The neighbourhood is well served by MUNI buses and BART, making it easy to reach other parts of San Francisco. Taxis and rideshares like Uber and Lyft are also readily available, providing convenient options for getting around.

Recommended Restaurants

Dining in the Tenderloin is diverse and reflects its cultural richness. Solo travellers can enjoy a meal at Saigon Sandwich, known for its delicious banh mi. Couples might prefer the intimate setting of Brenda's French Soul Food, which offers a cosy atmosphere and flavorful dishes. Families will appreciate the welcoming environment and diverse menu at The Chairman, perfect for a family-friendly dining experience. Groups can head to Farmhouse Kitchen Thai Cuisine, known for its vibrant décor and extensive menu, ideal for shared meals.

Hayes Valley

Scan the QR code to see the map of Hayes Valley

Hayes Valley is a vibrant and trendy neighbourhood in San Francisco known for its hip boutiques, artisanal cafes, and lively public spaces. It's a perfect blend of local charm and urban sophistication, offering plenty of attractions and activities for visitors.

Attractions

Hayes Valley is home to several notable attractions. Patricia's Green is a central park space that often features public art installations and is surrounded by cafes and shops. The San Francisco Symphony and the San Francisco Opera arc nearby, providing world-class performances. Octavia Art Gallery showcases contemporary art, while unique stores like Timbuk2 offer an eclectic shopping experience. For relaxation, Earthbody-MMassage San Francisco offers a range of spa treatments.

Getting There From Major Airports

From San Francisco International Airport (SFO), you can reach Hayes Valley by taking the BART to Civic Centre/UN Plaza Station, then walking or taking a short bus ride. This journey takes about 40 minutes. From Oakland International Airport (OAK), take the BART to Civic Centre/UN Plaza Station, followed by a walk or a short bus ride, totaling around 50 minutes. From Norman Y. Mineta San Jose International Airport (SJC), the trip involves taking the Caltrain to San Francisco, then a bus or taxi, which takes about 1.5 to 2 hours.

Accommodation Options

Hayes Valley offers a range of accommodations to suit different budgets. Sonder Hayes Valley is a modern option with stylish rooms and convenient amenities. For a boutique experience, the Inn at the Opera provides charming accommodations with a cultural touch. Budget travellers can find affordable options at nearby hostels or budget hotels, ensuring a comfortable stay close to the heart of the action.

Transportation Options

Navigating Hayes Valley is convenient due to its walkable streets and excellent public transportation options. The area is well served by MUNI buses, providing easy access to other parts of San Francisco. Taxis and rideshares like Uber and Lyft are also readily available, making it easy to get around.

Recommended Restaurants

Dining in Hayes Valley is a culinary delight. Solo travellers can enjoy a meal at Anina, known for its creative cocktails and vibrant atmosphere. Couples might prefer the intimate setting of Petit Crenn, offering a French-inspired dining experience. Families will appreciate the diverse menu at Souvla, serving delicious Greek dishes in a family-friendly setting. Groups can head to Rich Table for its innovative American cuisine and lively ambiance, perfect for shared dining experiences.

Japantown

Scan the QR code to see the map of Japantown

Japantown in San Francisco is a vibrant neighbourhood rich in culture, history, and Japanese heritage. This district offers an authentic slice of Japan within the heart of the city, making it a must-visit for anyone exploring San Francisco.

Attractions

Japantown is packed with attractions that showcase its unique character. The Japan Center Mall is the neighborhood's central hub, featuring a wide variety of shops, restaurants, and cultural goods. The Peace Plaza is a significant landmark with its iconic Peace Pagoda, a five-tiered concrete stupa gifted by San Francisco's sister city, Osaka. Visitors can relax at the Kabuki Springs and Spa, known for its traditional Japanese baths and serene environment. For those interested in literature and culture, the Kinokuniya Bookstore offers a vast selection of Japanese books, magazines, and gifts. Additionally, the AMC Kabuki 8 theater provides a modern movie-going experience with a touch of Japanese flair.

Getting There From Major Airports

From San Francisco International Airport (SFO), Japantown can be reached by taking the BART to Civic Centre/UN Plaza Station, followed by a short MUNI bus ride. This journey typically takes about 40 minutes. From Oakland International Airport (OAK), take the BART to Embarcadero Station, then transfer to a MUNI bus, totaling around 50 minutes. From Norman Y. Mineta San Jose International Airport (SJC), the trip involves taking the Caltrain to San Francisco, followed by a bus or taxi, which takes about 1.5 to 2 hours.

Accommodation Options

Japantown offers several accommodation options that cater to different budgets and preferences. For a luxurious stay, consider the Hotel Kabuki, which blends traditional Japanese design with modern amenities. Mid-range travellers might enjoy the Kimpton Buchanan Hotel, known for its comfortable rooms and proximity to key attractions. Budget-conscious travellers can find affordable accommodations at the nearby Queen Anne Hotel, which provides a charming and historic setting.

Transportation Options

Navigating Japantown is easy with its walkable layout and excellent public transportation. MUNI buses provide comprehensive coverage, making it simple to reach other parts of San Francisco. Taxis and rideshares like Uber and Lyft are also readily available, ensuring convenient travel around the district and beyond.

Recommended Restaurants

Japantown is a culinary delight with numerous dining options. Solo travellers can enjoy a meal at Marufuku Ramen, known for its rich and flavorful ramen bowls. Couples might prefer the intimate setting of OzaOza, offering an exquisite kaiseki dining experience. Families will appreciate the welcoming environment and diverse menu at Sushi Ran, perfect for a family-friendly dinner. Groups can head to Domo for its vibrant atmosphere and delicious izakaya-style dishes.

Presidio

Scan the QR code to see the map of Presidio

The Presidio is a sprawling, picturesque district in San Francisco known for its historical significance, natural beauty, and diverse recreational opportunities. Once a military post, this area now serves as a national park and offers visitors a unique blend of history, outdoor activities, and cultural experiences.

Attractions

The Presidio is home to numerous attractions that appeal to a wide range of interests. The Walt Disney Family

Museum provides a fascinating look into the life and legacy of Walt Disney. Crissy Field offers stunning views of the Golden Gate Bridge and is perfect for picnics, jogging, and kite flying. The Presidio Officers' Club is one of San Francisco's oldest buildings and now functions as a museum and cultural center. The Presidio Trust maintains a variety of trails, including the scenic Lobos Creek Valley Trail, which provides a serene nature experience. Presidio Tunnel Tops is a newly developed park area offering breathtaking views and family-friendly activities.

Getting There From Major Airports

From San Francisco International Airport (SFO), you can reach the Presidio by taking the BART to Montgomery Street Station, then transferring to a MUNI bus. This journey takes about 50 minutes. From Oakland International Airport (OAK), take the BART to Embarcadero Station, then transfer to a MUNI bus, totaling around an hour. From Norman Y. Mineta San Jose International Airport (SJC), the trip involves taking the Caltrain to San Francisco, followed by a bus or taxi, which takes about 1.5 to 2 hours.

Accommodation Options

The Presidio offers a range of accommodations that blend comfort with historical charm. The Lodge at the Presidio provides luxury accommodations with stunning views and close proximity to key attractions. For a more boutique experience, consider the Inn at the Presidio, which offers cosy rooms and a welcoming atmosphere.

Budget travellers can find affordable options at nearby hotels and motels, ensuring a comfortable stay within easy reach of the presidio's highlights.

Transportation Options

Exploring the Presidio is convenient, with several transportation options. The area is highly walkable, and numerous trails and paths make it ideal for hiking and biking. MUNI buses serve the area well, providing access to other parts of San Francisco. Taxis and rideshares like Uber and Lyft are also readily available for quick trips around the district.

Recommended Restaurants

Dining in the Presidio caters to various tastes and preferences. Solo travellers can enjoy a meal at The Commissary, known for its contemporary American cuisine with a Spanish flair. Couples might prefer the intimate setting of Arguello, which offers Mexican-inspired dishes and a vibrant atmosphere. Families will appreciate the diverse menu at Presidio Social Club, perfect for a family-friendly dining experience. Groups can head to Sessions at the Presidio, which features a lively atmosphere and an extensive selection of craft beers and innovative dishes.

Richmond District

Scan the QR code to see the map of Richmond District

The Richmond District in San Francisco is a sprawling and diverse neighbourhood known for its proximity to parks, rich cultural scene, and a variety of dining and entertainment options. It stretches from the serene Golden Gate Park to the lively Pacific Ocean, offering a mix of urban and natural attractions.

Attractions

The Richmond District is home to several notable attractions. Land's End is a scenic coastal trail offering breathtaking views of the Golden Gate Bridge and the rugged coastline. Lincoln Park features the stunning Palace of the Legion of Honour, an art museum with an impressive collection of European art. Clement Street is the district's bustling commercial hub, known for its eclectic mix of restaurants, shops, and bookstores. Golden Gate Park borders the district to the south and includes landmarks like the Conservatory of Flowers and the de Young Museum. The Balboa Theatre is a charming historic cinema that screens both classic and contemporary films.

Getting There From Major Airports

From San Francisco International Airport (SFO), you can reach the Richmond District by taking the BART to Civic Centre/UN Plaza Station, then transferring to a MUNI bus. This journey typically takes about 50 minutes. From Oakland International Airport (OAK), take the BART to Embarcadero Station and then switch to a MUNI bus, totaling around an hour. From Norman Y. Mineta San Jose International Airport (SJC), the trip involves taking the Caltrain to San Francisco, followed by a bus or taxi, which takes about 1.5 to 2 hours.

Accommodation Options

The Richmond District offers various accommodations suitable for different budgets. For a boutique experience, consider staying at the Hotel Drisco, which provides luxurious amenities and close proximity to major attractions. Mid-range travellers might enjoy the Geary Parkway Motel, which offers comfortable rooms and convenient access to public transportation. Budget travellers can find affordable options at nearby hostels and budget hotels, ensuring a comfortable stay close to the district's highlights.

Transportation Options

Navigating the Richmond District is straightforward, with several transportation options. The neighbourhood is well served by MUNI buses, which provide easy access to other parts of San Francisco. Walking and biking are also popular ways to explore the district, especially with its proximity to parks and scenic trails. Taxis and rideshares like Uber and Lyft are readily available for convenient travel.

Recommended Restaurants

Dining in the Richmond District caters to a variety of tastes. Solo travellers can enjoy a meal at B Star Bar, known for its delicious Asian fusion dishes. Couples might prefer the intimate setting of Mescolanza, which offers Italian cuisine in a cosy atmosphere. Families will appreciate the welcoming environment and diverse menu at Lokma, perfect for a family-friendly dining experience. Groups can head to Burma Superstar for its lively ambiance and flavorful Burmese dishes.

Sunset District

Scan the QR code to see the map of Sunset District

The Sunset District in San Francisco is a vast and diverse neighbourhood known for its residential charm, scenic parks, and proximity to the Pacific Ocean. It offers a peaceful retreat from the bustling city centre while still providing plenty of attractions and activities for visitors.

Attractions

The Sunset District is home to several notable attractions. Golden Gate Park borders the district to the north and includes must-see sites like the Conservatory of Flowers and the de Young Museum. Grand View Park offers panoramic views of the city and the ocean, making it a perfect spot for a peaceful hike. Spreckels Lake is a serene location for a leisurely walk or picnic. The San Francisco Women Artists Gallery showcases contemporary art from local female artists, adding a cultural touch to the neighborhood. For those looking to relax, Ocean Beach offers a long stretch of sand ideal for sunbathing, surfing, and enjoying the sunset.

Getting There From Major Airports

From San Francisco International Airport (SFO), you can reach the Sunset District by taking the BART to Daly City Station, followed by a short MUNI bus ride. This journey typically takes about 45 minutes. From Oakland International Airport (OAK), take the BART to Embarcadero Station and then switch to a MUNI bus, totaling around an hour. From Norman Y. Mineta San Jose International Airport (SJC), the trip involves taking the Caltrain to San Francisco, followed by a bus or taxi, which takes about 1.5 to 2 hours.

Accommodation Options

The Sunset District offers a variety of accommodations. SeaScape Inn provides budget-friendly rooms with easy access to the beach. For a boutique experience, consider Inn San Francisco, which blends historical charm with modern amenities. Mid-range travellers might enjoy the convenience of the Ocean Park Motel, which offers comfortable rooms and a retro vibe.

Transportation Options

Navigating the Sunset District is straightforward with its excellent public transportation options. The area is well served by MUNI buses and light rail, providing easy access to other parts of San Francisco. Walking and biking are also popular ways to explore the district, especially with its proximity to parks and scenic trails. Taxis and rideshares like Uber and Lyft are readily available for convenient travel.

Recommended Restaurants

Dining in the Sunset District caters to a variety of tastes. Solo travellers can enjoy a meal at Judahlicious, known for its healthy and delicious vegan dishes. Couples might prefer the intimate setting of Hook Fish Co., offering fresh seafood in a cosy atmosphere. Families will appreciate the welcoming environment and diverse menu at Sunset Cantina, perfect for a family-friendly dining experience. Groups can head to the Outerlands for its vibrant ambiance and inventive dishes, ideal for shared dining experiences.

Noe Valley

Scan the QR code to see the map of Noe Valley

Noe Valley is a charming and upscale neighbourhood in San Francisco, known for its beautiful Victorian homes, family-friendly atmosphere, and vibrant community life. It's a delightful area that combines the feel of a small village with the amenities of a bustling city.

Attractions

Noe Valley offers several attractions that capture its unique charm. The main commercial thoroughfare, 24th Street, is lined with boutique shops, cafes, and restaurants, making it a great place for a leisurely stroll. Sanchez Street is another notable area, known for its historic walking tours and picturesque architecture. Art enthusiasts will appreciate Lola's Art Gallery, which features local artists. For those who enjoy unique shopping experiences, Chocolate Covered is a must-visit shop offering a variety of delicious treats.

Getting There From Major Airports

From San Francisco International Airport (SFO), you can reach Noe Valley by taking the BART to Glen Park Station, followed by a short MUNI bus ride or a walk. This journey typically takes about 35 minutes. From Oakland International Airport (OAK), take the BART to Embarcadero Station, transfer to the J-Church MUNI line, and get off at the 24th Street Mission Station, totaling around 50 minutes. From Norman Y. Mineta San Jose International Airport (SJC), the trip involves taking the Caltrain to San Francisco, followed by a bus or taxi, which takes about 1.5 to 2 hours.

Accommodation Options

Noe Valley offers several accommodation options for different budgets. The Parker Guest House, located nearby, provides a comfortable and welcoming atmosphere with beautiful gardens. For a more budget-friendly option, consider staying at the Noe's Nest Bed and Breakfast, which offers a cosy and unique lodging experience.

Transportation Options

Navigating Noe Valley is easy with its excellent public transportation options. The neighbourhood is well served by MUNI buses and the J-Church streetcar line, which provide convenient access to other parts of San Francisco. Walking and biking are also popular ways to explore the area, thanks to its pleasant streets and manageable hills. Taxis and rideshares like Uber and Lyft are readily available for quick trips around the city.

Recommended Restaurants

Dining in Noe Valley is a treat with its diverse culinary offerings. Solo travellers can enjoy a meal at Philz Coffee, known for its custom-blended coffee drinks. Couples might prefer the intimate setting of Contigo, offering delicious Spanish tapas. Families will appreciate the welcoming environment and diverse menu at Patxi's Pizza, perfect for a family-friendly dining experience. Groups can head to Firefly Restaurant for its lively atmosphere and inventive dishes, ideal for shared dining experiences.

Bernal Heights

Scan the QR code to see the map of Bernal Heights

Bernal Heights is a quaint and charming neighbourhood in San Francisco, known for its picturesque views, quiet streets, and vibrant community. Nestled atop a hill, it offers a perfect mix of urban living and nature, making it a delightful spot for both residents and visitors.

Attractions

Bernal Heights is best known for Bernal Heights Park, which offers panoramic views of San Francisco and beyond. The park is ideal for hiking, picnicking, and enjoying the sunset. Precita Park is another local favourite, providing a more intimate green space perfect for family outings and dog walks. The neighbourhood's main street, Cortland Avenue, is lined with unique shops, cafes, and restaurants, giving visitors a taste of the local lavor. For art enthusiasts, Inclusions Gallery showcases works by local artists, adding a cultural touch to your visit.

Getting There From Major Airports

From San Francisco International Airport (SFO), you can reach Bernal Heights by taking the BART to Glen Park Station, followed by a short bus ride or walk. This journey typically takes about 30 minutes. From Oakland International Airport (OAK), take the BART to Embarcadero Station and transfer to the J-Church MUNI line, getting off at the 24th Street Mission Station, totaling around 50 minutes. From Norman Y. Mineta San Jose International Airport (SJC), the trip involves taking the Caltrain to San Francisco, followed by a bus or taxi, taking about 1.5 to 2 hours.

Accommodation Options

Bernal Heights offers several charming accommodations. For a boutique experience, consider staying at Parker Guest House, which offers comfortable rooms and a homey atmosphere. Budget travellers might enjoy Noe's Nest Bed and Breakfast, which provides a cosy and affordable stay.

Transportation Options

Exploring Bernal Heights is easy, with several transportation options. The neighbourhood is highly walkable, and MUNI buses provide convenient access to other parts of San Francisco. Taxis and rideshares like Uber and Lyft are readily available, ensuring easy travel around the area.

Recommended Restaurants

Dining in Bernal Heights is a culinary adventure. Solo travellers can enjoy a meal at Red Hill Station, known for its fresh seafood. Couples might prefer the intimate setting of 3rd Cousin, which offers a Michelin-rated dining experience. Families will appreciate the welcoming environment at Bernal Star, which is perfect for a family-friendly dining experience. Groups can head to Piqueos for its vibrant atmosphere and flavorful Peruvian dishes.

Glen Park

Scan the QR code to see the map of Glen Park

Glen Park is a picturesque and cosy neighbourhood in San Francisco, offering a blend of urban living and natural beauty. Known for its charming village-like feel and accessibility to green spaces, Glen Park is a favourite among locals and visitors looking for a serene yet vibrant atmosphere.

Attractions

Glen Park boasts several attractions that showcase its unique character. Glen Canyon Park is a highlight, offering almost four miles of hiking trails through a lush, natural setting with wildflowers, Eucalyptus trees, and native wildlife such as owls and hawks. The park also features a baseball field and tennis courts, making it a great spot for outdoor activities.

Billy Goat Hill is another popular attraction, known for its breathtaking views of the city and a famous rope swing that offers a thrilling way to enjoy the scenery. Nearby, the Walter Haas Playground provides a perfect space for families, with play structures, basketball courts, and a dog run.

For those interested in cultural experiences, Glen Park hosts the annual Glen Park Festival, a one-day event featuring live music, a parade, games, and activities for children. The festival emphasises community spirit and family-friendly fun, usually taking place in April.

Getting There From Major Airports

From San Francisco International Airport (SFO), Glen Park is easily accessible by taking the BART to Glen Park Station, which is a quick 30-minute ride. From Oakland International Airport (OAK), take the BART to Glen Park Station, which involves a transfer at Embarcadero Station, totaling around 50 minutes. From Norman Y. Mineta San Jose International Airport (SJC), the journey involves taking the Caltrain to San Francisco, followed by a bus or taxi, taking about 1.5 to 2 hours.

Accommodation Options

Glen Park offers several comfortable accommodation options. For a boutique experience, consider staying at Parker Guest House, which offers cosy rooms and beautiful gardens. Budget travellers might enjoy the Noe's Nest Bed and Breakfast, which provides a charming and affordable lodging experience nearby.

Transportation Options

Navigating Glen Park is straightforward with its excellent public transportation options. The BART and MUNI buses provide easy access to other parts of San Francisco. Walking and biking are also popular ways to explore the area, thanks to its pleasant streets and scenic trails. Taxis and rideshares like Uber and Lyft are readily available for convenient travel.

Recommended Restaurants

Dining in Glen Park is a treat with its variety of culinary offerings. Solo travelers can enjoy a meal at Pebbles Cafe, known for its great coffee, sandwiches, and Brazilian acai bowls. Couples might prefer the intimate setting of Gialina Pizzeria, offering some of the best thin-crust pizzas in the city. Families will appreciate the welcoming environment at Le P'tit Laurent, perfect for a family-friendly dining experience. Groups can head to Manzoni, which features vibrant Italian dishes and a lively atmosphere, ideal for shared meals.

Excelsior District

Scan the QR code to see the map of Excelsior District

The Excelsior District in San Francisco is a diverse and vibrant neighbourhood known for its rich cultural heritage and strong community spirit. It offers a unique blend of residential charm, historic significance, and bustling commercial activity, making it a fascinating place for both locals and visitors.

Attractions

The Excelsior District boasts several notable attractions that highlight its cultural diversity and community-oriented atmosphere. John McLaren Park is the second-largest park in San Francisco, offering a variety of recreational activities, including hiking trails, picnic areas, and the Jerry Garcia Amphitheater, which hosts various events and performances. Mission Street, the main commercial drag, is lined with diverse eateries, shops, and colorful street art, reflecting the neighborhood's multicultural character.

Another significant attraction is the Excelsior Playground, which provides a great spot for families with children to enjoy outdoor activities. The Excelsior Branch Library is not only a place for reading but also a community hub offering various programs and events for all ages. Balboa Park is also nearby, featuring sports fields, a swimming pool, and a historic movie theater.

Getting There From Major Airports

From San Francisco International Airport (SFO), you can reach the Excelsior District by taking the BART to Balboa Park Station, followed by a short bus ride or walk. This journey typically takes about 30-40 minutes. From Oakland International Airport (OAK), take the BART to Balboa Park Station, with a transfer at Embarcadero Station, totaling around 50 minutes. From Norman Y. Mineta San Jose International Airport (SJC), the trip involves taking the Caltrain to San Francisco, followed by a bus or taxi, taking about 1.5 to 2 hours.

Accommodation Options

The Excelsior District offers several accommodation options. The Mylo Hotel provides comfortable and affordable rooms with convenient access to public transportation. For a more unique experience, consider staying at a local bed and breakfast or an Airbnb, where you can enjoy the neighborhood's residential charm and hospitality.

Transportation Options

Getting around the Excelsior District is easy with its excellent public transportation options. The area is well-served by MUNI buses, including the 14-Mission line, which runs along Mission Street and connects to other parts of San Francisco. Walking and biking are also popular ways to explore the district, thanks to its pedestrian-friendly streets and scenic routes. Taxis and rideshares like Uber and Lyft are readily available for convenient travel.

Recommended Restaurants

Dining in the Excelsior District is a culinary adventure with a variety of options reflecting the neighborhood's diversity. Solo travelers can enjoy a meal at Excelsior Coffee, known for its great coffee and pastries. Couples might prefer the intimate setting of The Dark Horse Inn, offering a cozy atmosphere and comfort food. Families will appreciate the welcoming environment at Little Joe's Pizza, perfect for a family-friendly dining experience. Groups can head to Gentilly, which features vibrant New Orleans-inspired cuisine and a lively atmosphere, ideal for shared dining experiences.

Bayview-Hunters Point

Scan the QR code to see the map of Bayview-Hunters Point

Bayview-Hunters Point is a vibrant and culturally rich neighborhood in the southeastern part of San Francisco. Known for its historical significance and diverse community, this district offers unique attractions and dining.

Attractions

Bayview-Hunters Point is home to several notable attractions. Candlestick Point State Recreation Area is a highlight, offering over 170 acres of protected parkland with picnic areas, fishing piers, and hiking trails. This area is also popular for windsurfing and provides stunning views of the bay. Another significant site is the San Francisco Shipyard, currently undergoing redevelopment to transform the former naval shipyard into a vibrant community with residential, commercial, and recreational spaces.

The Bayview Opera House Ruth Williams Memorial Theatre, built in 1888, serves as a community center hosting music concerts, art performances, and cultural exhibitions. Additionally, the Quesada Gardens in the heart of Bayview showcases beautiful murals and community gardens, reflecting the neighborhood's artistic spirit and community pride.

Getting There From Major Airports

From San Francisco International Airport (SFO), Bayview-Hunters Point can be reached by taking the BART to the Balboa Park Station, followed by a MUNI bus ride. This journey typically takes about 40 minutes. From Oakland International Airport (OAK), take the BART to Embarcadero Station and transfer to the T-Third MUNI light rail line, totaling around 50 minutes. From Norman Y. Mineta San Jose International Airport (SJC), the trip involves taking the Caltrain to San

Francisco, followed by a bus or taxi, taking about 1.5 to 2 hours.

Accommodation Options

Accommodation options in Bayview-Hunters Point include a mix of boutique hotels and budget-friendly stays. While there are limited traditional hotel options within the district itself, nearby neighborhoods like Mission Bay and Potrero Hill offer a range of accommodations that provide easy access to Bayview. Options include the Marriott Marquis for a more luxurious stay or Travelodge by Wyndham for a budget-friendly choice.

Transportation Options

Navigating Bayview-Hunters Point is straightforward with several transportation options. The area is well-served by the MUNI T-Third light rail line, providing direct access to downtown San Francisco. MUNI buses also operate extensively throughout the neighborhood, offering convenient connections to other parts of the city. Taxis and rideshares like Uber and Lyft are readily available for more flexible travel.

Recommended Restaurants

Dining in Bayview-Hunters Point reflects the neighborhood's diversity. Solo travelers can enjoy a meal at Radio Africa & Kitchen, known for its Afro-Mediterranean cuisine. Couples might prefer the cozy atmosphere of Gratta Wines, offering locally produced wines and a charming setting. Families will appreciate the friendly environment and diverse menu at Old Skool Cafe, a youth-run supper club. Groups can head to Speakeasy Brewery for its lively ambiance, craft beers, and regular events.

Twin Peaks

Scan the QR code to see the map of Twin Peaks

Twin Peaks is a must-visit district in San Francisco, known for its breathtaking panoramic views of the city. Standing at over 900 feet above sea level, these two adjacent peaks offer visitors unparalleled vistas of San

Francisco's skyline, the Bay Area, and beyond. The area is a favorite spot for both tourists and locals, especially at sunset when the views are particularly stunning.

Attractions

The main attraction of Twin Peaks is, of course, the incredible views. The Twin Peaks Summit provides a 360-degree perspective of the city, making it an ideal location for photography and sightseeing. The Christmas Tree Point lookout is another popular spot, offering slightly different but equally impressive vistas. For those interested in a bit more adventure, the area also features several hiking trails, such as the Twin Peaks Loop, which takes you through the natural landscape of the peaks.

Getting There From Major Airports

From San Francisco International Airport (SFO), you can reach Twin Peaks by taking the BART to Civic Center Station, then transferring to the MUNI bus 37, which will take you close to the peaks. The total journey takes about 40 minutes. From Oakland International Airport (OAK), the trip involves taking the BART to Embarcadero Station and then the MUNI bus 37, totaling around 50 minutes. From Norman Y. Mineta San Jose International Airport (SJC), the trip involves taking the Caltrain to San Francisco, followed by a bus or taxi, taking about 1.5 to 2 hours.

Accommodation Options

Twin Peaks does not have many accommodation options directly within the area, but nearby neighborhoods like Castro and Noe Valley offer several choices. Consider Beck's Motor Lodge in the Castro, which provides comfortable accommodations with easy access to Twin Peaks. For more budget-friendly options, Parker Guest House offers charming rooms and a cozy atmosphere.

Transportation Options

Navigating Twin Peaks is straightforward with several transportation options. The area is accessible by the MUNI bus 37, which provides a direct route from nearby neighborhoods. Walking and biking are also popular ways to explore the area, thanks to its scenic trails. Taxis and rideshares like Uber and Lyft are readily available for more flexible travel.

Recommended Restaurants

Dining options near Twin Peaks cater to various tastes. Solo travelers can enjoy a meal at Twin Peaks Tavern, known for its historic significance and great atmosphere. Couples might prefer the intimate setting of Mama Ji's, offering delicious Chinese cuisine. Families will appreciate the welcoming environment at Frances, perfect for a family-friendly dining experience. Groups can head to L'Ardoise Bistro for its vibrant atmosphere and French dishes, ideal for shared meals.

Twin Peaks offers a unique blend of natural beauty, community charm, and urban convenience, making it a perfect addition to any San Francisco itinerary.

San Francisco's neighbourhood each offer a unique and captivating experience. Every neighborhood has something special to explore. These diverse areas collectively paint a rich tapestry of the city's identity, making San Francisco a truly extraordinary destination for all types of travelers.

CHAPTER 3

Getting There And Around

Flights To San Francisco

San Francisco is a major hub for both domestic and international flights, making it easily accessible from virtually anywhere in the world. The city is served by three major airports: San Francisco International Airport (SFO), Oakland International Airport (OAK), and Norman Y. Mineta San Jose International Airport (SJC). Each of these airports offers a range of services and connections, ensuring a smooth journey to and from the Bay Area.

San Francisco International Airport (SFO)

San Francisco International Airport (SFO) is the primary airport serving the city and is located approximately 13 miles south of downtown San Francisco. SFO is one of the busiest airports in the United States, offering numerous domestic and international flights. Major airlines such as United Airlines, Delta, American Airlines, and Southwest operate extensive networks from SFO, providing frequent flights to and from major cities across the United States and the world.

SFO has four terminals: Terminal 1 (Harvey Milk Terminal), Terminal 2, Terminal 3, and the International Terminal. Each terminal is equipped with a variety of amenities, including dining options, shops, and lounges.

The airport also offers free Wi-Fi throughout its premises.

For international travellers, SFO serves as a gateway to destinations in Asia, Europe, Oceania, and the Americas. Airlines such as British Airways, Lufthansa, Singapore Airlines, and Cathay Pacific operate regular flights to and from SFO. The airport's International Terminal is equipped with modern facilities to handle a high volume of passengers, ensuring efficient customs and immigration processes.

Oakland International Airport (OAK)

Oakland International Airport (OAK) is located across the bay from San Francisco, approximately 20 miles from downtown. While smaller than SFO, OAK is a convenient alternative for travellers, particularly those coming from or heading to destinations within the western United States. Southwest Airlines is a major carrier at OAK, offering frequent flights to cities across the U.S. Alaska Airlines, Spirit Airlines, and Allegiant Air also operate numerous routes from this airport.

OAK consists of two terminals, Terminal 1 and Terminal 2, both of which offer a range of services and amenities, including dining options, shops, and free Wi-Fi. The airport is known for its efficiency and shorter security lines, making it a popular choice for many travellers.

Norman Y. Mineta San Jose International Airport (SJC)

Norman Y. Mineta San Jose International Airport (SJC) is located about 45 miles south of San Francisco. SJC is particularly convenient for travellers visiting the southern parts of the Bay Area, including Silicon Valley. The airport is well-connected with domestic flights operated by major carriers like Alaska Airlines, Southwest Airlines, and Delta. International airlines such as ANA, British Airways, and Lufthansa provide services to key global destinations.

SJC has two terminals, Terminal A and Terminal B, which offer a variety of amenities, including dining and shopping options, as well as free Wi-Fi throughout the airport. The airport's compact size and efficient layout make it easy to navigate, providing a hassle-free travel experience.

Getting to San Francisco from the Airports

Each airport offers various transportation options to reach downtown San Francisco. From SFO, travellers can take the Bay Area Rapid Transit (BART) directly from the airport to downtown, which takes about 30 minutes. Shuttle services, taxis, rideshares, and car rentals are also available.

From OAK, travellers can take the BART from the Oakland Coliseum Station, which is connected to the airport by a dedicated shuttle. This journey takes around 40 minutes. Alternatively, taxis, rideshares, and car rentals are available for those who prefer private transportation.

From SJC, the Caltrain offers service to downtown San Francisco, though travellers will need to take a shuttle or taxi to the nearest Caltrain station in Santa Clara. The total journey time is approximately 1.5 to 2 hours. Taxis, rideshares, and car rentals are also available directly from the airport.

San Francisco's accessibility via three major airports ensures that travellers have multiple options for their journey. The variety of airlines and services at SFO, OAK, and SJC cater to all travel needs, making the Bay Area a convenient and attractive destination for visitors from around the globe. Ensuring a smooth arrival, these airports provide efficient transport links to the heart of San Francisco, setting the stage for an enjoyable visit to this iconic city.

By planning your flight to San Francisco and knowing your options, you can ensure a smooth and enjoyable start to your visit.

Arriving in San Francisco

Arriving in San Francisco is an exciting experience, marked by the city's iconic landscapes, diverse neighbourhoods, and rich culture. Whether flying into San Francisco International Airport (SFO), Oakland International Airport (OAK), or Norman Y. Mineta San

Jose International Airport (SJC), travellers can expect a smooth transition into the city.

Arrival at San Francisco International Airport (SFO)

San Francisco International Airport (SFO) is the largest airport in the Bay Area, situated about 13 miles south of downtown San Francisco. Upon landing, passengers are greeted with a range of amenities and services. The airport has four terminals: Terminals 1, 2, 3, and the International Terminal. Each terminal is well-equipped with dining options, shops, lounges, and free Wi-Fi.

After disembarking, travellers will go through customs and immigration if arriving on an international flight. The process is efficient, with clear signage and helpful staff to assist passengers. Luggage claim areas are conveniently located near the exits.

Ground Transportation from SFO

Travellers have multiple options for getting to downtown San Francisco from SFO. The Bay Area Rapid Transit (BART) provides a direct connection from the airport to various parts of the city. The BART station is located in the International Terminal, making it accessible from all other terminals via AirTrain, SFO's free inter-terminal train service.

Alternatively, taxis and rideshare services like Uber and Lyft are available outside each terminal. For those preferring a more private ride, car rental services are located at the Rental Car Centre, accessible via the

AirTrain. Shuttle services and buses also operate from the airport, providing convenient and affordable transport to hotels and other destinations.

Arrival at Oakland International Airport (OAK)

Oakland International Airport (OAK) is situated approximately 20 miles from downtown San Francisco. This airport is a smaller but more efficient alternative, known for its shorter security lines and quick baggage claim. Upon arrival, passengers can find various amenities, including dining options, shops, and free Wi-Fi.

Ground Transportation from OAK

To reach San Francisco from OAK, travellers can take the BART from the airport's dedicated BART station. A shuttle service connects the terminal to the Coliseum/Oakland Airport BART station. From there, passengers can take a train directly into San Francisco.

Taxis and rideshare services are also available outside the terminals, providing convenient transport to the city. Additionally, several shuttle services operate between OAK and San Francisco, offering a balance between cost and convenience. Car rental services are available within the airport, allowing travellers to explore the Bay Area at their own pace.

Arrival at Norman Y. Mineta San Jose International Airport (SJC)

Norman Y. Mineta San Jose International Airport (SJC) is about 45 miles south of San Francisco. It is particularly convenient for travellers heading to the southern parts of the Bay Area, including Silicon Valley. The airport has two terminals, A and B, each offering a range of amenities such as dining, shopping, and free Wi-Fi.

Ground Transportation from SJC

Travellers can reach San Francisco from SJC by taking the Caltrain, which connects San Jose to San Francisco. A shuttle or taxi ride from the airport to the nearest Caltrain station is required. This journey offers scenic views of the Bay Area and is a popular choice for those who prefer not to drive.

Taxis and rideshare services are readily available at SJC, providing a direct route to San Francisco. Car rental services are also available at the airport, offering flexibility for those who wish to drive.

Tips for a Smooth Arrival

Regardless of the airport, it is important to have a plan for transportation and accommodation upon arrival. Pre-booking transport or knowing the available options can save time and reduce stress. Having the address of your destination handy and being aware of the general layout of the airport will also contribute to a smoother experience.

Travellers should remain aware of their belongings, especially in busy areas like baggage claim and transport hubs. Using official transport services and avoiding unlicensed taxis or rideshares can help ensure safety and avoid potential scams.

Arriving in San Francisco sets the stage for an exciting and memorable visit. The city's efficient transport systems and welcoming atmosphere make the transition from airport to city both easy and enjoyable, allowing travellers to start their adventure in the Bay Area on a high note.

Public Transportation

San Francisco boasts one of the most comprehensive and efficient public transportation systems in the United States. With various modes of transport, including buses, light rail, cable cars, and ferries, getting around the city is convenient and accessible. Understanding how to navigate this system can greatly enhance your travel experience.

San Francisco Municipal Transportation Agency (SFMTA)

The San Francisco Municipal Transportation Agency (SFMTA), also known as Muni, operates the city's public transit system. Muni includes buses, light rail vehicles, historic streetcars, and iconic cable cars, offering extensive coverage across San Francisco.

Muni buses and light rail

Muni buses and light rail vehicles are the backbone of public transit in San Francisco. Buses cover almost every corner of the city, making it easy to reach various destinations. The light rail system, consisting of seven lines (J, K, L, M, N, S, and T), serves key areas, including downtown, the Financial District, and neighbourhoods like the Castro and Sunset. Muni Metro trains run underground in the downtown area and above ground in other parts of the city, providing quick and reliable service.

Historic Streetcars

The F Market & Wharves line features historic streetcars from around the world, running along Market Street and the Embarcadero to Fisherman's Wharf. These streetcars not only provide transportation but also offer a nostalgic journey through the city's transit history.

Cable Cars

San Francisco's cable cars are a quintessential part of the city's charm. Three lines (Powell-Mason, Powell-Hyde, and California Street) traverse the steep hills of the city, offering stunning views and a unique ride experience. While cable cars are a popular tourist attraction, they are also a practical way to navigate some of the city's most challenging terrain.

Bay Area Rapid Transit (BART)

The Bay Area Rapid Transit (BART) system connects San Francisco with neighbouring cities in the Bay Area, including Oakland, Berkeley, and San Jose. BART is a fast and efficient way to travel to and from San Francisco International Airport (SFO) and Oakland International Airport (OAK). Within the city, BART serves several key stations, including Embarcadero, Montgomery, Powell, and Civic Centre, making it easy to transfer to Muni services.

Caltrain

Caltrain provides commuter rail service along the San Francisco Peninsula, connecting the city with San Jose and other South Bay communities. With stops at key locations like Millbrae, Redwood City, and Palo Alto, Caltrain is an excellent option for those travelling to and from Silicon Valley. The northern terminus at 4th and King Street in San Francisco is easily accessible by Muni buses and light rail.

Ferries

The San Francisco Bay Ferry and Golden Gate Ferry systems offer scenic and convenient routes across the bay. Ferries connect San Francisco with destinations such as Sausalito, Tiburon, Larkspur, and Alameda. The main ferry terminal at the Ferry Building on the Embarcadero is a hub of activity, featuring shops, restaurants, and farmers markets.

Clipper Card

The Clipper Card is a reusable contactless smart card used for electronic transit fare payment in the San Francisco Bay Area. It can be used on Muni, BART, Caltrain, and most other public transit services in the region. The card makes transfers between different systems seamless and offers discounted fares compared to cash payments. Clipper Cards can be purchased and reloaded at numerous locations, including ticket machines at BART and Muni stations, retail outlets, and online.

Accessibility

San Francisco's public transportation system is designed to be accessible to everyone, including those with disabilities. Most Muni buses and trains are equipped with ramps or lifts for wheelchair access. Additionally, BART and Caltrain stations have elevators and other facilities to assist passengers with mobility impairments. Accessible seating and audible announcements ensure that all passengers can travel comfortably and safely.

Safety Tips

While San Francisco's public transportation system is generally safe, it's important to stay aware of your surroundings. Keep personal belongings secure and avoid displaying valuable items. During late hours, travel with companions if possible and use well-lit stations and stops.

San Francisco's robust public transportation system offers a convenient and cost-effective way to explore the city and the surrounding Bay Area. Understanding how to navigate buses, light rail, historic streetcars, cable cars, BART, Caltrain, and ferries can enhance your visit and provide a seamless travel experience. Public transportation in San Francisco is a reliable and enjoyable way to get around.

Car Rentals

Renting a car in San Francisco can be a convenient way to explore the city and its surrounding areas at your own pace. Having a car provides flexibility and freedom. However, it's important to understand the process, costs, and practicalities to ensure a smooth rental experience.

Car Rental Agencies

San Francisco offers a wide variety of car rental agencies, both at the airports and within the city. Major companies such as Hertz, Avis, Enterprise, Budget, and National operate at San Francisco International Airport (SFO), Oakland International Airport (OAK), and Norman Y. Mineta San Jose International Airport (SJC). These agencies also have numerous locations throughout the city, making it convenient to pick up and drop off your rental car.

Booking a Car

Booking a rental car can be done online through the rental agency's website, through third-party booking sites, or directly at the rental location. Booking in advance is recommended, especially during peak travel seasons, as it ensures availability and often provides better rates. When booking, you'll need to provide your driver's license, a credit card for the rental deposit, and choose the type of vehicle that best suits your needs.

Types of Vehicles

Car rental agencies in San Francisco offer a range of vehicles to suit different preferences and needs. Compact and economy cars are popular choices for navigating the city's narrow streets and finding parking. If you're travelling with a group or have a lot of luggage, consider renting a mid-size or full-size car, SUV, or minivan. For a more luxurious experience or special occasions, premium vehicles and convertibles are also available.

Insurance and Additional Coverage

When renting a car, it's essential to understand the insurance options available. Basic rental rates usually include minimum liability coverage, but additional coverage such as a collision damage waiver (CDW), personal accident insurance, and theft protection can be purchased for extra protection. Check if your personal car insurance or credit card offers rental car coverage to avoid paying for duplicate insurance.

Fuel Policy

Car rental companies typically offer different fuel policies. The most common is the full-to-full policy, where you pick up the car with a full tank of gas and must return it full. This policy ensures you only pay for the fuel you use. Alternatively, some companies offer pre-purchase fuel options, allowing you to return the car without refuelling, though this is often more expensive.

Driving and parking in San Francisco

Driving in San Francisco can be challenging due to its steep hills, narrow streets, and heavy traffic. However, it offers a unique way to experience the city's diverse neighbourhoods and scenic views. Be mindful of parking regulations, as parking can be difficult to find and expensive. The city has metered street parking, parking garages, and public parking lots. Be sure to read all parking signs carefully to avoid fines.

Exploring beyond San Francisco

Having a rental car allows you to explore beyond the city limits. Popular day trips include driving to the coastal towns of Monterey and Carmel, visiting the vineyards of Napa Valley, or hiking in Muir Woods National Monument. The iconic Pacific Coast Highway offers breathtaking views and is a favourite route for travellers heading south towards Big Sur.

Returning the Car

When returning the rental car, ensure you adhere to the rental company's return policy. Return the car on time to avoid late fees and in the same condition as when you picked it up. If you opted for the full-to-full fuel policy, refuel the car before returning it. Most rental agencies provide a receipt and final bill upon return.

Renting a car in San Francisco provides the flexibility to explore the city and its surrounding areas at your own pace. By understanding the rental process, insurance options, and driving conditions, you can ensure a smooth and enjoyable experience.

Bike and Scooter Rentals

Renting a bike or scooter in San Francisco is an excellent way to explore the city's diverse neighbourhoods, scenic waterfronts, and iconic landmarks. With dedicated bike lanes, scenic routes, and numerous rental options, these eco-friendly modes of transport offer both convenience and an immersive travel experience.

Bike Rentals

San Francisco is well-equipped for cycling, with numerous bike rental shops and services scattered throughout the city. Companies like Blazing Saddles, Bay City Bike, and Wheel Fun Rentals provide a range of bicycles, including standard road bikes, electric bikes, and tandem bikes. Many rental shops are conveniently located near popular tourist areas such as Fisherman's Wharf, making it easy to pick up a bike and start your journey.

When renting a bike, you'll typically be provided with a helmet, a lock, and a map of recommended routes. It's important to wear a helmet and follow traffic rules for safety. Popular bike routes include the Golden Gate Bridge to Sausalito, which offers stunning views of the bay and the bridge, and the Embarcadero, which provides a flat and scenic ride along the waterfront.

Scooter Rentals

Electric scooters have become a popular way to navigate San Francisco's urban landscape. Companies like Lime, Bird, and Spin offer dockless electric scooters that can be rented via mobile apps. These scooters are perfect for short trips and provide a fun and efficient way to get around the city.

To rent a scooter, download the respective app, locate a scooter using the app's map, and scan the QR code on the scooter to unlock it. The rental cost typically includes a base fee and a per-minute charge. Electric scooters are best suited for relatively flat areas and short commutes. They can be a great option for quickly getting to nearby attractions, commuting between meetings, or simply enjoying a leisurely ride.

Safety and Regulations

Safety is paramount when renting bikes and scooters in San Francisco. Cyclists should always use bike lanes where available and obey traffic signals. The city's hills can be challenging, so it's crucial to be cautious and use proper braking techniques. For scooter users, wearing a helmet and following local regulations are mandatory. Scooters should be parked in designated areas and not block sidewalks or access points.

San Francisco has specific regulations for electric scooters to ensure safety and orderliness. Riders must be at least 18 years old and possess a valid driver's license. Scooters are not allowed on sidewalks and should be ridden in bike lanes or on streets with a speed limit of 25 mph or less.

Exploring San Francisco by Bike or Scooter

Exploring San Francisco by bike or scooter allows you to experience the city in a unique and interactive way. You can ride through iconic locations like the Golden Gate Park, which offers over 1,000 acres of green space, museums, and gardens. The park's extensive network of paths and trails makes it ideal for biking.

The Mission District, with its vibrant murals and diverse food scene, is another great area to explore on a bike or scooter. Valencia Street in the Mission has bike lanes and is known for its bike-friendly atmosphere. The Presidio, a former military base turned national park, offers scenic routes with breathtaking views of the Golden Gate Bridge and the Pacific Ocean.

Practical Tips

When renting a bike or scooter, consider the duration of your rental. Many companies offer hourly, daily, and multi-day rates, so choose the option that best fits your plans. Additionally, check if the rental service provides roadside assistance in case of a breakdown.

For a more structured experience, guided bike tours are available. These tours often include a knowledgeable guide who can share insights about the city's history, culture, and landmarks while navigating popular routes. This can be a great way to explore the city if you're unfamiliar with the area or prefer a group setting.

Environmental Impact

Choosing to rent a bike or scooter is not only convenient but also environmentally friendly. It reduces your carbon footprint and helps alleviate traffic congestion. San Francisco encourages the use of these green transportation options as part of its commitment to sustainability and reducing greenhouse gas emissions.

Renting a bike or scooter in San Francisco offers a flexible, fun, and eco-friendly way to explore the city. Whether you're riding across the Golden Gate Bridge, cruising along the Embarcadero, or navigating through the city's diverse neighbourhoods, these modes of transport provide a memorable and enjoyable experience. By understanding the rental process, safety regulations, and best routes, you can make the most of your time in San Francisco while contributing to a cleaner, greener environment.

Walking

San Francisco is known for its walkability, with many neighbourhoods best explored on foot. Walking allows you to experience the city's unique character, from the bustling streets of Chinatown to the serene paths of Golden Gate Park. Be prepared for steep hills, and wear comfortable shoes for the best experience.

Taxis and Rideshares

Taxis and rideshare services like Uber and Lyft are readily available throughout San Francisco. These services are convenient for short trips or when public transportation options are limited. They can be hailed via mobile apps and provide door-to-door service.

Tips for Navigating the City

Plan your route.

Use apps like Google Maps or Transit to plan your journey. These apps provide real-time updates on public transport schedules and suggest the best routes.

Avoid Rush Hour

Traffic can be heavy during peak times (7-9 AM and 4-6 PM). If possible, travel outside these hours to avoid congestion.

Stay Aware

Keep an eye on your belongings, especially in crowded areas. San Francisco is generally safe, but it's always good to be vigilant.

Layer Up

The city's weather can change quickly. Dress in layers to stay comfortable throughout the day.

Enjoy the View

Take time to enjoy the scenic views, whether you're on a cable car, ferry, or walking through a park.

By understanding the various transportation options and planning your routes, you can navigate San Francisco with ease and make the most of your visit. The city's extensive public transport system, scenic routes, and walkable neighborhoods ensure that you can explore all its unique offerings comfortably and conveniently.

CHAPTER 4

Accomodations

Finding a place to stay in San Francisco is easy, with a variety of recommendations available. You can choose from elegant hotels with stunning views or budget-friendly hostels. Whatever your preference, you'll find comfortable and welcoming accommodations throughout the city.

Luxury Hotels

San Francisco boasts some of the most exquisite luxury hotels, offering an unmatched combination of comfort, elegance, and top-notch service. Below are descriptions of some of the finest options.

Fairmont San Francisco

Located at 950 Mason Street, the Fairmont San Francisco is an iconic luxury hotel known for its historic grandeur and impeccable service.

How to Get There

From San Francisco International Airport (SFO), take the BART to Powell Street Station, then take a short cable car ride or taxi to the hotel. From Oakland International Airport (OAK), BART to Powell Street Station, and then a cable car or taxi. From Norman Y.

Mineta San Jose International Airport (SJC), take the Caltrain to San Francisco, followed by a taxi.

Website

Fairmont

Amenities

The hotel features 606 individually decorated rooms, including 62 elegant suites with views of the city and the bay. Amenities include a fitness centre, spa, fine dining at the Laurel Court Restaurant & Bar, and a rooftop garden.

Cost

Rooms start at around $400 per night.

Transportation Options

Valet parking, nearby public transportation, including cable cars, taxis, and rideshares.

Nearby Attractions

Union Square, Fisherman's Wharf, Chinatown, and the Cable Car Museum.

Recommended Restaurants

Nob Hill Café (Italian), Tacorea (Mexican), and Akiko's Sushi Bar.

The Ritz-Carlton, San Francisco

Situated atop Nob Hill at 600 Stockton Street, The Ritz-Carlton offers a serene retreat in the heart of the city.

How to Get There

From SFO, take BART to Montgomery Street Station, then take a short walk or taxi ride. From OAK, take BART to Montgomery Street Station. From SJC, take the Caltrain to San Francisco, then a taxi.

Website

The Ritz-Carlton, San Francisco

Amenities

The hotel offers luxurious rooms, a renowned restaurant, a full-service spa, and a fitness center. Guests can enjoy the club-level services and professional staff.

Cost

Starting rates are around $500 per night.

Transportation Options

Valet parking, easy access to public transportation.

Nearby Attractions

Chinatown, Union Square, and the Ferry Building.

Recommended Restaurants

Tacorea (Mexican), Bouche (French), and City View Restaurant (Chinese).

The St. Regis San Francisco

Located at 125 Third Street, The St. Regis combines timeless elegance with modern amenities, perfect for discerning travellers.

How to Get There

From SFO, take BART to Montgomery Street Station, then take a short walk. From OAK, take BART to Montgomery Street Station. From SJC, take the Caltrain to San Francisco, then a taxi.

Website

[The St. Regis San Francisco Luxury Hotel](#)

Amenities

The hotel features 260 refined rooms and suites, an American restaurant, the St. Regis Bar, and a luxurious spa. Rooms offer indulgent beds, spacious workstations, and large bathrooms with soaking tubs and rainforest showers.

Cost

Rooms start at around $450 per night.

Transportation Options

Valet parking, proximity to public transportation.

Nearby Attractions

San Francisco Museum of Modern Art (SFMOMA), Yerba Buena Gardens, and the Ferry Building.

Recommended Restaurants

Fogo de Chão Brazilian Steakhouse, Mourad (Moroccan), and The Grove (Yerba Buena).

Four Seasons Hotel San Francisco at Embarcadero

This hotel, located at 222 Sansome Street, rises above downtown, offering breathtaking views from its top floors.

How to Get There

From SFO, take BART to Embarcadero Station, then take a short walk. From OAK, take BART to Embarcadero Station. From SJC, take the Caltrain to San Francisco, then a taxi.

Website

San Francisco at Embarcadero, Four Seasons Hotel

Amenities

The hotel features luxurious rooms with modern amenities, a top-notch fitness centre, and various dining options. It is renowned for its exceptional service and cleanliness.

Cost

Rooms start at $400 per night.

Transportation Options

Valet parking is close to public transportation.

Nearby Attractions

Union Square, Ferry Building, and Fisherman's Wharf.

Recommended Restaurants

Kokkari Estiatorio (Mediterranean), Perbacco (Italian), and Yank Sing (Chinese).

Tips

Avoid making loud noises, especially late at night. Respect the hotel's smoking and pet policies. Do not take hotel property like towels or bathrobes as souvenirs.

Pack comfortable shoes for exploring, a jacket for the often chilly evenings, and any personal toiletries you prefer. Bringing a power bank for your devices can also be useful.

Booking directly through the hotel's website often provides the best rates and access to exclusive deals. Use public transportation where possible to avoid the hassle of parking and to reduce your environmental footprint.

Staying in one of San Francisco's luxury hotels guarantees an exceptional experience, from the finest amenities to prime locations near the city's top attractions. Enjoy the ultimate in comfort and service as you explore everything this iconic city has to offer.

Boutique Hotels

San Francisco's boutique hotels offer a unique blend of charm, comfort, and personalised service. Below are some of the best boutique hotels in the city.

Lodge at the Presidio

The Lodge at the Presidio, located at 105 Montgomery Street, provides a serene and picturesque retreat within the historic Presidio National Park.

How to Get There

From San Francisco International Airport (SFO), take the BART to Montgomery Street Station, then take a taxi or rideshare to the hotel. From Oakland International Airport (OAK), BART to Embarcadero Station, then a taxi or rideshare. From Norman Y. Mineta San Jose

International Airport (SJC), take a train to San Francisco, followed by a taxi.

Website

Lodge at the Presidio | San Francisco Hotel

Amenities

The lodge offers 42 rooms, many with views of the Golden Gate Bridge. Amenities include complimentary continental breakfast, evening wine and cheese receptions, a fire pit, and access to hiking trails.

Cost

Rooms start at around $350 per night.

Transportation Options

Free shuttle service within the Presidio, access to public buses, and ample parking.

Nearby Attractions

Golden Gate Bridge, Crissy Field, Walt Disney Family Museum.

Recommended Restaurants

Presidio Social Club (American), Sessions at the Presidio (New American).

Hotel Griffon

Hotel Griffon is located at 155 Steuart Street along the Embarcadero, providing easy access to the waterfront and downtown attractions.

How to Get There

From SFO, take BART to Embarcadero Station, then take a short walk. From OAK, BART to Embarcadero Station. From SJC, take the take the Caltrain to San Francisco, then a taxi or rideshare.

Website

[Hotel Griffon: A Boutique Hotel in San Francisco](#)

Amenities

The hotel offers well-appointed rooms with city and bay views, complimentary Wi-Fi, and on-site dining at Perry's on the Embarcadero.

Cost

Rooms start at around $200 per night.

Transportation Options

Close to BART and MUNI stations, taxis, and rideshares.

Nearby Attractions

Ferry Building Marketplace, Embarcadero Centre, Bay Bridge.

Recommended Restaurants

Boulevard (American), Hog Island Oyster Co. (Seafood), The Slanted Door (Vietnamese).

Hotel Del Sol

Hotel Del Sol, located at 3100 Webster Street, celebrates California's vibrant culture with a colourful and relaxed atmosphere.

How to Get There

From SFO, take BART to Montgomery Street Station, then a taxi or rideshare. From OAK, BART to Montgomery Street Station. From SJC, take the take the Caltrain to San Francisco, then a taxi.

Website

Hotel Del Sol San Francisco

Amenities

The hotel features spacious rooms, a heated outdoor pool, free breakfast, and a pet-friendly policy.

Cost

Rooms start at around $150 per night.

Transportation Options

Accessible by public buses, taxis, and rideshares.

Nearby Attractions

Marina District, Golden Gate Bridge, Fort Mason.

Recommended Restaurants

Pacific Catch (seafood), Delarosa (Italian), and Blackwood (Thai Fusion).

Tips

Avoid making excessive noise, particularly during late hours. Respect non-smoking policies and be considerate of other guests by keeping shared spaces tidy.

Bring comfortable walking shoes, a light jacket for San Francisco's variable weather, and a power bank for your devices. Also, carry your ID and a credit card for incidental expenses.

Booking directly through the hotel's website can offer the best rates and special deals. Utilise public transportation to avoid parking hassles and embrace the local experience.

By choosing one of these boutique hotels, you can enjoy a personalised and charming stay in San Francisco with easy access to top attractions, dining, and entertainment options. Enjoy the comfort and character of these unique accommodations as you explore all that the city has to offer.

Budget-Friendly Accommodations

San Francisco is known for its high living costs, but there are still many budget-friendly hotels that offer comfort, convenience, and great amenities. Here are some of the top budget-friendly hotels in the city, along with essential details to make your stay enjoyable.

Castle Inn

Castle Inn, located at 1565 Broadway Street, provides affordable accommodation in a great location.

How to Get There

From San Francisco International Airport (SFO), take BART to Powell Street Station, then a bus or taxi to the hotel. From Oakland International Airport (OAK), take BART to Powell Street Station, then a bus or taxi. From Norman Y. Mineta San Jose International Airport (SJC), take the Caltrain to San Francisco, then a taxi.

Website

Castle Inn San Francisco

Amenities

Free parking, complimentary continental breakfast, free Wi-Fi, refrigerator, and microwave in rooms.

Cost

Rooms start at around $150 per night.

Transportation Options

Easily accessible by bus, taxi, and rideshare.

Nearby Attractions

Fisherman's Wharf, Lombard Street, and Chinatown.

Recommended Restaurants

Swan Oyster Depot (seafood), House of Prime Rib (steakhouse).

The Metro Hotel

The Metro Hotel, located at 319 Divisadero Street, is known for its charm and affordability. This boutique hotel offers a cosy and welcoming atmosphere, making it a favourite among budget travellers seeking an authentic San Francisco experience.

How to Get There

From San Francisco International Airport (SFO), take the BART to Civic Centre Station, then transfer to the

MUNI bus line 7, which stops close to the hotel. From Oakland International Airport (OAK), take the BART to Civic Centre Station and follow the same MUNI route. From Norman Y. Mineta San Jose International Airport (SJC), take the Caltrain to San Francisco, then a taxi or rideshare to the hotel.

Website

The Metro Hotel in Haight-Ashbury

Amenities

The Metro Hotel offers comfortable rooms with free Wi-Fi, a garden patio, and complimentary coffee and tea. The hotel prides itself on providing a homey feel with friendly service.

Cost

Rooms start at around $170 per night.

Transportation Options

Public buses (MUNI), taxis, and rideshares.

Nearby Attractions

Alamo Square, Painted Ladies, and Haight-Ashbury.

Recommended Restaurants

Nopa (New American), Little Star Pizza (Pizza), and Brenda's Meat & Three (Southern).

Tips

Avoid making excessive noise in your room, and respect the shared spaces. Some hotels have a no-smoking policy.

Bring comfortable walking shoes, a light jacket for the cool evenings, and any personal toiletries you prefer.

Booking directly through the hotel's website often provides the best rates and access to exclusive deals. Additionally, third-party booking sites like TripAdvisor can offer competitive rates and reviews to help you make your decision.

These budget-friendly options ensure that you can enjoy a comfortable stay in San Francisco without spending a fortune. With convenient locations, excellent amenities, and easy access to public transportation, these hotels offer everything you need for a memorable visit to the city.

Hostels

San Francisco offers a variety of hostel accommodations, perfect for budget-conscious travellers who still seek comfort and a sense of community. Here are the recommended hostels in the city.

HI San Francisco Downtown Hostel

Located at 312 Mason Street, the HI San Francisco Downtown Hostel is a favourite among travellers for its central location and welcoming atmosphere.

How to Get There

From San Francisco International Airport (SFO): Take the BART from SFO to Powell Street Station. The hostel is a 4-minute walk from the station.

From Oakland International Airport (OAK): Take the BART from OAK to Embarcadero Station, then transfer to Powell Street Station.

From Norman Y. Mineta San Jose International Airport (SJC): Take the Caltrain to San Francisco, then a short taxi or rideshare to the hostel.

Website

HI San Francisco Downtown Hostel

Amenities

Free Wi-Fi, complimentary breakfast, a fully equipped kitchen, a contemporary lounge, a media room, a 24-hour front desk, self-serve laundry, and baggage storage.

Cost

Dorm beds start around $40 per night, with private rooms starting around $120.

Transportation Options

Easily accessible by BART, MUNI, taxis, and rideshares.

Nearby Attractions

Union Square, Powell and Market Cable Car Turnaround, San Francisco Playhouse, and the San Francisco Magic Theatre.

Recommended Restaurants

Taylor Street Coffee Shop (American), Lapisara Eatery (Asian), and Fino Bar & Ristorante (Italian).

ITH Pacific Tradewinds Hostel

Situated at 680 Sacramento Street, ITH Pacific Tradewinds Hostel is known for its social environment and prime location near the Financial District.

How to Get There

From San Francisco International Airport (SFO): Take the BART to Montgomery Street Station, then a short walk to the hostel.

From Oakland International Airport (OAK): Take the BART to Montgomery Street Station.

From Norman Y. Mineta San Jose International Airport (SJC): Take the Caltrain to San Francisco, then a taxi or rideshare.

Website

Pacific Tradewinds

Amenities

Free Wi-Fi, complimentary breakfast, communal kitchen, lounge area, lockers, and organised social events.

Cost

Dorm beds start at around $40 per night.

Transportation Options

Close to BART, MUNI, and easily accessible by taxis and rideshares.

Nearby Attractions

Chinatown, the Transamerica Pyramid, North Beach, and the Ferry Building.

Recommended Restaurants

House of Nanking (Chinese), Tadich Grill (Seafood), and Ramen Underground (Japanese).

Tips

Do not leave personal items unattended in communal areas, and adhere to the hostel's quiet hours.

Bring a lock for lockers, personal toiletries, and earplugs if you're a light sleeper.

It is best to book directly through the hostel's website or through reputable booking platforms to secure the best rates and availability.

Be respectful of shared spaces and fellow travelers. Clean up after yourself in kitchens and bathrooms.

Always use the provided lockers to secure valuables, and be mindful of the hostel's entry and exit policies.

Hostels in San Francisco offer a great way to meet fellow travellers and stay in central locations without breaking the bank. By choosing to stay in these budget-friendly accommodations, you can enjoy the city's vibrant atmosphere and numerous attractions while saving money for experiences and activities.

Vacation Rentals

San Francisco offers an excellent selection of vacation rentals that provide a cosy, home-like atmosphere perfect for families, groups, and solo travellers alike.

Noe's Nest Bed and Breakfast

Located in the charming Noe Valley neighbourhood, Noe's Nest Bed and Breakfast offers a delightful stay in a historic Victorian house, complete with a welcoming atmosphere and unique decor.

How to Get There

From San Francisco International Airport (SFO): Take the BART to Glen Park Station, then take a short taxi or rideshare to the B&B.

From Oakland International Airport (OAK): Take the BART to Glen Park Station, then a short taxi or rideshare.

From Norman Y. Mineta San Jose International Airport (SJC): Take the Caltrain to San Francisco, then a taxi or rideshare.

Website

Noe's Nest: Bed and Breakfast San Francisco

Amenities

Offers uniquely decorated rooms with flat-screen TVs, free Wi-Fi, private marble bathrooms, and a generous daily buffet breakfast. Some suites include a spa bath and garden views.

Cost

Rates start at around $190 per night.

Transportation Options

Easily accessible by public transportation with nearby BART and Muni stops. Taxis and rideshares are readily available.

Nearby Attractions

Dolores Park, Mission District murals, and numerous boutique shops and cafes.

Recommended Restaurants

Foreign Cinema, Beretta, and Tartine Bakery.

Chateau Tivoli Bed and Breakfast

Chateau Tivoli Bed and Breakfast is a beautifully restored mansion located in the historic Alamo Square district. This B&B combines historic charm with modern comforts.

How to Get There

From SFO: Take the BART to Civic Centre Station, then a short taxi or rideshare.

From OAK: Take the BART to Civic Centre Station, then a short taxi or rideshare.

From SJC: Take the Caltrain to San Francisco, then a taxi or rideshare.

Website

Chateau Tivoli

Amenities

Features individually decorated rooms with antique furnishings, free Wi-Fi, and a complimentary breakfast. Some rooms have private bathrooms, while others share bathrooms.

Cost

Rates start at around $250 per night.

Transportation Options

Well-connected by public transportation, including buses and taxis. Parking is available for guests.

Nearby Attractions

Alamo Square and the Painted Ladies, Hayes Valley shopping and dining, and the Haight-Ashbury district.

Recommended Restaurants

Nopa, Brenda's French Soul Food, and Souvla

Tips

Avoid making excessive noise, especially late at night, to respect neighbors. Adhere to the property's rules regarding cleanliness and waste disposal. Do not rearrange furniture or tamper with fixtures without permission.

Pack comfortable walking shoes, a light jacket for San Francisco's variable weather, and personal toiletries. Bringing a power bank for your devices is also advisable.

Booking directly through the property's website or a trusted platform like Airbnb often provides the best rates and terms. Utilise public transportation to avoid parking hassles and fully immerse yourself in the local experience.

Staying in a vacation rental in San Francisco ensures a comfortable and memorable experience with easy access to the city's top attractions and dining options. Enjoy the unique charm and flexibility that vacation rentals offer, providing a home-away-from-home experience in this vibrant city.

Family-Friendly Accommodations

San Francisco is an excellent destination for families, offering a variety of family-friendly hotels that cater to the needs of all ages. Here are some top recommendations.

Argonaut Hotel

The Argonaut Hotel, located at 495 Jefferson Street, is a beloved family-friendly hotel in the heart of Fisherman's Wharf. Its nautical theme and historic charm make it a favourite among travellers with children.

How to Get There

From San Francisco International Airport (SFO), take the BART to Embarcadero Station, then transfer to the F-Market Streetcar. From Oakland International Airport (OAK), take the BART to Embarcadero Station and then the F-Market Streetcar. From Norman Y. Mineta San Jose International Airport (SJC), take the Caltrain to San Francisco, then a taxi or rideshare to the hotel.

Website

Argonaut Hotel

Amenities

The hotel offers spacious rooms with two queen beds suitable for families, complimentary bike rentals, a fitness centre, and pet-friendly accommodations. The $35 daily amenities fee includes access to the Maritime National Historical Park, board games, and scavenger hunts.

Cost

Rooms start at around $350 per night.

Transportation Options

Close to cable cars, buses, and ferries.

Nearby Attractions

Ghirardelli Square, Pier 39, and the Hyde Street Cable Car.

Recommended Restaurants

Buena Vista Café (American), Scoma's (Seafood), and Blue Mermaid (Seafood).

Hotel Zephyr

Hotel Zephyr is a vibrant, family-friendly hotel located at 250 Beach Street in Fisherman's Wharf. It offers plenty of activities for children and proximity to many of the city's best attractions.

How to Get There

From SFO, take the BART to Embarcadero Station, then transfer to the F-Market Streetcar. From OAK, take the BART to Embarcadero Station and then the F-Market Streetcar. From SJC, take the Caltrain to San Francisco, then a taxi or rideshare.

Website

Hotel Zephyr San Francisco

Amenities

The hotel features indoor and outdoor play areas, including fire pits, shuffleboards, and a game room with pool tables and ping pong. Rooms are equipped with comfortable bedding, coffee makers, and mini-fridges.

Cost

Rooms start at around $250 per night.

Transportation Options: Close to public transportation, including cable cars and buses.

Nearby Attractions

Pier 39, Aquarium of the Bay, and Fisherman's Wharf.

Recommended Restaurants

Fog Harbour Fish House (seafood), Boudin Bakery & Café (American), and Alioto's (seafood).

The Omni San Francisco Hotel

The Omni San Francisco Hotel, located at 500 California Street in the Financial District, is known for its luxurious accommodations and excellent service.

How to Get There

From SFO, take BART to Montgomery Street Station, then take a short walk. From OAK, take BART to

Montgomery Street Station. From SJC, take the Caltrain to San Francisco, then a taxi or rideshare.

Website

The Omni San Francisco Hotel

Amenities

The hotel features spacious rooms with connecting options, babysitting services, and special activity backpacks for kids. There is also an on-site restaurant and room service.

Cost

Rates start at approximately $300 per night.

Transportation Options

The hotel is well served by public transportation, taxis, and rideshares.

Nearby Attractions

Chinatown, the Embarcadero, and the Ferry Building.

Recommended Restaurants

Kokkari Estiatorio (mediterranean), Tadich Grill (seafood), and Yank Sing (dim sum).

Tips

Avoid making excessive noise, especially late at night, to respect other guests. Follow the hotel's policies on cleanliness and waste disposal. Do not let children play unsupervised in common areas or pools.

Pack comfortable walking shoes, a light jacket for San Francisco's variable weather, and personal toiletries. Consider bringing snacks, a first-aid kit, and entertainment for children, such as books or tablets.

Booking directly through the hotel's website often provides the best rates and access to special deals. Utilise public transportation to avoid parking hassles and fully immerse yourself in the local experience. Enjoy the amenities and services that cater specifically to families, making your stay in San Francisco both comfortable and memorable.

The Best Neighbourhoods to Stay in

San Francisco is a city of distinct and vibrant neighbourhoods, each offering its own unique charm and amenities. Choosing the right neighbourhood can greatly enhance your experience.

Union Square

Union Square is the bustling centre of San Francisco's shopping, dining, and entertainment scene. Staying here puts you at the heart of the city's action, surrounded by high-end retail stores, department stores, theatres, art galleries, and an array of dining options. This central location makes it an ideal base for exploring the city, with excellent public transportation connections including BART, Muni buses, and cable cars. The convenience of having major attractions like Chinatown, the Financial District, and the Moscone Centre within walking distance makes Union Square a prime choice for visitors.

Locals appreciate Union Square for its vibrancy and the multitude of activities it offers. It's a lively area where both tourists and residents can enjoy shopping, dining, and cultural events. The central location and accessibility make it a favoured spot for both short-term and long-term stays.

Fisherman's Wharf

Fisherman's Wharf is a top destination for families and first-time visitors, known for its picturesque waterfront views and iconic attractions. Staying at Fisherman's Wharf offers easy access to popular sites such as Pier 39, Ghirardelli Square, and the Maritime National Historical Park. The area is famous for its seafood restaurants and family-friendly activities. Visitors can enjoy stunning views of Alcatraz Island and the Golden Gate Bridge. The historic cable cars, Muni buses, and ferries provide excellent transportation options to explore other parts of the city.

While Fisherman's Wharf is seen as a tourist hotspot, its charm and the freshness of the seafood available are undeniable. The picturesque waterfront and proximity to major attractions make it a top choice for visitors seeking a quintessential San Francisco experience.

Nob Hill

Nob Hill is synonymous with elegance and history, offering a refined San Francisco experience. Known for its upscale hotels, historic mansions, and stunning views, Nob Hill provides a quieter, more relaxed atmosphere compared to the bustling Union Square. The neighbourhood is home to iconic landmarks such as Grace Cathedral and luxurious hotels like the Fairmont and the InterContinental Mark Hopkins. The area's elevated location offers breathtaking views of the city and the bay, and the historic cable cars provide a charming and convenient way to get around.

Nob Hill is appreciated for its historic significance, stunning architecture, and serene environment. It offers a blend of old-world charm and modern amenities, making it a favoured spot for those seeking a more sophisticated stay.

The Mission District

The Mission District is celebrated for its vibrant culture, colourful murals, and eclectic dining options. This neighbourhood offers a rich cultural experience with a blend of history, art, and modernity. The area is home to some of San Francisco's best restaurants, bars, and cafes, providing a diverse culinary experience. The neighbourhood's murals and street art are world-renowned, and the bustling atmosphere provides a true taste of San Francisco life. The mission is well connected by public transportation, making it easy to explore other parts of the city.

The Mission District is loved for its authenticity and vibrant arts scene. The diverse food offerings and lively nightlife make it a popular choice for both locals and visitors looking to immerse themselves in the city's cultural fabric.

Pacific Heights

Pacific Heights is known for its luxurious homes, stunning views of the Golden Gate Bridge, and serene atmosphere. This neighbourhood offers a peaceful retreat from the hustle and bustle of the city while still being close to major attractions. The area's beautiful parks, such as Lafayette Park and Alta Plaza Park, provide excellent spots for relaxation and enjoying the views. Pacific Heights is dotted with high-end boutiques and gourmet restaurants, adding to its upscale appeal.

Pacific Heights is valued for its elegance, safety, and community feel. The clean streets and beautiful architecture make it a desirable place to live and visit, offering a residential charm that is hard to match.

North Beach

North Beach, also known as San Francisco's Little Italy, is famous for its Italian heritage, lively atmosphere, and historic landmarks. Staying in North Beach puts you close to attractions like Coit Tower, Washington Square

Park, and a plethora of Italian restaurants and cafes. The area's nightlife is vibrant, with numerous bars, clubs, and live music venues. It's conveniently located near Chinatown and the Financial District, providing easy access to different parts of the city.

North Beach is cherished for its rich history and cultural significance. The neighbourhood's dining scene and lively streets are beloved by residents, making it a perfect choice for those who enjoy vibrant nightlife and cultural experiences.

Choosing the right neighbourhood in San Francisco can greatly enhance your stay, offering convenience, comfort, and a unique local experience. Each of these neighbourhoods offers something special, ensuring that your visit to San Francisco is memorable and tailored to your preferences. Enjoy exploring the city's diverse and dynamic neighbourhoods, each offering its own slice of what makes San Francisco a world-renowned destination.

CHAPTER 5

Top Attractions

San Francisco is a city teeming with iconic landmarks, vibrant culture, and breathtaking scenery. Its top attractions provide a diverse array of experiences. This guide aims to highlight the best of what the city has to offer, ensuring that every visitor finds something to inspire and captivate them.

Golden Gate Bridge

The Golden Gate Bridge, an iconic symbol of San Francisco, stretches 1.7 miles across the Golden Gate Strait, connecting the city to Marin County. This architectural marvel, painted in its distinctive international orange, has been captivating visitors since its completion in 1937.

Scan the QR code to see more information from the map of Golden Gate Bridge

The main access point to the Golden Gate Bridge for visitors is via the Golden Gate Bridge Welcome Centre, located at 201 Fort Mason, San Francisco, CA 94123. Due to the limited parking at the bridge plaza, especially on weekends and holidays, it's recommended to use public transportation. Various bus routes, including the Golden Gate Transit (Route 130), can take you directly to the bridge from downtown San Francisco.

Alternatively, ride-sharing services like Uber and Lyft are convenient options.

The bridge is open to vehicle and bicycle traffic 24/7. Pedestrian access is allowed during daylight hours, generally from sunrise to sunset. The Welcome Centre is open daily from 9:00 a.m. to 6:00 p.m., except on Thanksgiving and Christmas.

Visitors walking or cycling on the bridge should adhere to safety regulations, including staying within designated paths and yielding to others as necessary. Cyclists must observe a speed limit of 15 mph on the sidewalks and slow to 5 mph around the towers. Additionally, the bridge's sidewalks close one hour earlier during Pacific Daylight Time.

The Golden Gate Bridge Welcome Centre provides a wealth of information, exhibits on the bridge's history and construction, and a range of souvenirs. Nearby, the Round House Café offers refreshments with stunning views of the bridge. For restrooms, facilities are located across the visitor plaza, near the parking lot.

Visiting the bridge is free for pedestrians and cyclists. Motorists pay a southbound toll when driving into San Francisco, with fees processed electronically. Various tours, including walking and biking tours, range from approximately $40 to $160 per person.

Visitors can enjoy walking or biking across the bridge, which typically takes 45–60 minutes one way. The views from the bridge are spectacular, offering panoramas of the bay, city skyline, and Marin Headlands. The weather can be unpredictable, with foggy mornings often giving way to clear afternoons, so dressing in layers is advisable.

At the Welcome Centre, you can delve into the bridge's history through interactive exhibits and see authentic relics such as rivets and hard hats from its construction. Free walking tours are available on Thursdays and Sundays, providing deeper insights into the bridge's significance. Photography enthusiasts will find numerous vantage points, such as Battery East, the Golden Gate Overlook, and the Pacific Overlook, ideal for capturing the bridge's grandeur.

During your visit, consider exploring the adjacent Golden Gate National Recreation Area, which offers hiking trails and scenic vista points. The Presidio, located at the southern end of the bridge, features additional historical sites and outdoor activities.

With its rich history and stunning vistas, the Golden Gate Bridge remains a must-see attraction for anyone visiting San Francisco.

Alcatraz Island

Alcatraz Island, known as "The Rock," is a small island located in San Francisco Bay, about 1.25 miles from the northern shore of San Francisco. It was once the site of a federal prison that housed some of America's most notorious criminals, including Al Capone and Robert Stroud, the "Birdman of Alcatraz." Today, Alcatraz is a popular tourist attraction managed by the National Park Service, offering a fascinating glimpse into its storied past as a military fort, prison, and site of Native American occupation.

Scan the QR code to see more information from the map of Alcatraz Island

To visit Alcatraz Island, you need to take a ferry operated by Alcatraz City Cruises. The ferry departs from Pier 33, located along San Francisco's northern waterfront, near Fisherman's Wharf. It's advisable to book tickets in advance through the Alcatraz City Cruises website or by calling (415) 981-7625, as they often sell out weeks ahead, especially during peak tourist seasons. The ferry ride takes about 15 minutes each way, and it's recommended to arrive at Pier 33 at least 30 minutes before your scheduled departure time.

Alcatraz Island is open daily, with the first ferry departing at 8:45 a.m. The island is closed on Thanksgiving, Christmas, and New Year's Day. There are a variety of tour options available, including day tours, night tours, and behind-the-scenes tours. Day tour tickets are priced at $41 for adults, $25 for children aged 5–11, and $38 for seniors aged 62 and older. Family packages are also available.

When you arrive on the island, you'll find a range of activities to keep you engaged. The primary attraction is the self-guided audio tour of the former prison, which is included in the ticket price. This award-winning tour, narrated by former inmates and guards, provides a vivid account of life on Alcatraz. Visitors can explore the cellhouse, the dining hall, and other significant areas at their own pace. Additionally, there are several ranger-led programmes and special events, such as garden tours and historical presentations, which are included with your ticket.

The island offers spectacular views of the San Francisco skyline, the Golden Gate Bridge, and the Bay. Photography enthusiasts will find numerous vantage points for capturing stunning shots. While there are no food services on the island itself, the ferry has a snack bar where you can purchase light refreshments. Eating is only allowed at designated picnic areas near the dock.

Visitors should prepare for a lot of walking, often on steep hills. Comfortable shoes are a must, and it's advisable to dress in layers as the weather can be quite variable, with strong winds and fog common even in summer. Remember to bring essentials like water, sun protection, and a jacket. The island has limited restroom facilities, located at the dock and the top of the island.

A trip to Alcatraz Island is an immersive experience that offers insight into a unique chapter of American history. For more detailed information and to plan your visit, check out the National Park Service's Alcatraz page and the Alcatraz City Cruises website.

Fisherman's Wharf

Fisherman's Wharf, a vibrant waterfront neighbourhood in San Francisco, is a bustling hub of activity that perfectly blends the city's rich maritime history with modern attractions. Originally a hub for the local fishing industry in the 19th century, it has evolved into one of San Francisco's most popular tourist destinations, drawing millions of visitors each year.

Fisherman's Wharf is located along Jefferson Street between Hyde and Powell Streets. It's easily accessible by various forms of public transportation, including the historic cable cars, MUNI buses, and streetcars. For those driving, be prepared for limited parking and consider using a taxi or rideshare service to avoid the hassle.

While the area itself is open 24/7, most attractions, shops, and restaurants operate from around 8:00 a.m. to

10:00 p.m. It's best to check the specific hours for each attraction or restaurant you plan to visit.

Fisherman's Wharf is known for its lively atmosphere, with street performers and local vendors adding to the charm. Visitors are encouraged to respect the local customs, such as not feeding the sea lions and keeping the area clean by using designated trash bins.

The area is well-equipped with various services, including public restrooms, information centres, and ample dining options ranging from quick bites to sit-down seafood feasts. The Fisherman's Wharf Welcome Centre provides maps, brochures, and helpful tips for visitors.

Exploring Fisherman's Wharf can be enjoyed on any budget. Entry to the area is free, and there are plenty of affordable dining and entertainment options. For a more structured experience, guided tours and cruises are available, with prices typically ranging from $40 to $100 per person.

Visitors can expect a bustling atmosphere with plenty of sights and sounds. The area offers a range of activities, such as:

Dining

Savour fresh seafood like Dungeness crab and clam chowder in sourdough bread bowls from local eateries like Alioto's and Scoma's. For dessert, indulge in the treats at Ghirardelli Square..

Attractions

Visit Pier 39 to see the famous sea lions, explore the historic ships at Hyde Street Pier, or take a tour of the USS Pampanito, a World War II submarine. The area also features attractions like the Aquarium of the Bay, the San Francisco Maritime National Historical Park, and the quirky Musee Mecanique..

Shopping

The wharf is dotted with souvenir shops and boutiques where you can find unique gifts and local crafts.

Entertainment

Street performers are a staple at Fisherman's Wharf, providing entertainment for visitors throughout the day. For a unique experience, consider taking a ride on a GoCar, a GPS-guided storytelling vehicle, or joining a Segway tour to explore the area in a fun and novel way.

For those interested in maritime history, Fisherman's Wharf is a gateway to several educational experiences. The Maritime Museum and the SS Jeremiah O'Brien Liberty ship offer deeper insights into San Francisco's naval past. Additionally, several bay cruises depart from the wharf, offering scenic views of the Golden Gate Bridge, Alcatraz Island, and the city skyline.

Pier 39

Pier 39, located in the heart of San Francisco's Fisherman's Wharf, is a bustling waterfront marketplace and entertainment hub that offers a unique blend of shopping, dining, and attractions. This popular destination provides breathtaking views of San Francisco Bay, including iconic landmarks such as the Golden Gate Bridge, Alcatraz Island, and the Bay Bridge.

Scan the QR code to see more information from the map of Pier 39

Pier 39 is situated at Beach Street and the Embarcadero, just two blocks east of Fisherman's Wharf. The pier is easily accessible via public transportation, including the historic F-Market & Wharves streetcar, MUNI buses, and the Powell-Mason cable car line. For those driving, there is a multi-level parking garage located directly across the street from the entrance plaza, open 24 hours a day.

The attractions, shops, and restaurants at Pier 39 typically operate from 10:00 a.m. to 9:00 p.m., though some restaurants may open earlier for breakfast and close later for dinner. It's always a good idea to check with individual establishments for their specific hours of operation.

Visitors to Pier 39 are encouraged to enjoy the lively atmosphere while adhering to basic etiquette, such as not feeding the sea lions and keeping the area clean by disposing of trash properly. Pier 39 is a family-friendly environment, so respectful behaviour is expected.

Pier 39 offers a variety of services to ensure a comfortable visit. These include public restrooms, ATMs, and a range of dining options, from quick bites to full-service restaurants. The pier also features a five-acre waterfront park and a 300-berth marina.

Visiting Pier 39 is free, making it accessible to everyone. However, dining, shopping, and some attractions will incur costs. Budget-friendly options are available, but visitors should be prepared for higher prices at some restaurants and shops.

Pier 39 is a vibrant destination with a wide array of activities to enjoy. Visitors can expect:

Sea Lion Centre

One of the main attractions at Pier 39 is the Sea Lion Centre, where you can watch and learn about the playful sea lions that have made the pier their home since 1990.

Aquarium of the Bay

This engaging aquarium showcases the diverse marine life of the San Francisco Bay Area, featuring over 20,000 marine animals and interactive exhibits.

Carousel

The vintage carousel is a hit with children and offers a whimsical ride with beautiful views of the bay.

Street Performers

Talented street performers entertain the crowds with music, magic, and other captivating acts throughout the day.

Shopping and Dining

Pier 39 boasts over 60 specialty shops and a variety of dining options. You can savour local specialties like clam chowder in sourdough bread bowls and fresh Dungeness crab, or enjoy a meal at one of the upscale restaurants offering stunning bay views.

Bay Cruises

Several operators offer scenic cruises from Pier 39, providing panoramic views of San Francisco's waterfront landmarks, including the Golden Gate Bridge and Alcatraz Island.

Pier 39 also hosts seasonal events and festivals, adding to its lively and festive atmosphere. Pier 39 promises a memorable experience filled with entertainment, shopping, and spectacular views.

Golden Gate Park

Scan the QR code to see more information from the map of Golden Gate Park

Golden Gate Park, spanning over 1,017 acres in San Francisco, is an urban oasis offering a mix of natural beauty and cultural attractions. Created in the 1870s by field engineer William Hammond Hill and master gardener John McLaren, the park transformed an unpromising area into one of the city's most beloved green spaces. Today, it ranks as the third most-visited urban park in the United States, attracting millions of visitors annually.

Golden Gate Park stretches from Stanyan Street to the Great Highway, with key entrances at 501 Stanyan Street and several points along Lincoln Way. Public transportation options include MUNI buses (routes 5, 7, 21, and 28) and the N-Judah light rail. If driving, there are several parking areas, but using public transport or biking is recommended to avoid congestion.

The park is open daily from 5:00 a.m. to midnight. However, individual attractions within the park, such as museums and gardens, have their own operating hours. For example, the California Academy of Sciences and the de Young Museum are generally open from 9:30 a.m. to 5:00 p.m., with extended hours on certain days.

Visitors should adhere to park rules to maintain its beauty and tranquility. This includes staying on designated paths, not feeding wildlife, and respecting the park's flora. Specific areas may have additional rules, such as the Japanese Tea Garden's prohibition on picnicking within its grounds.

Golden Gate Park is equipped with numerous amenities, including restrooms, picnic areas, and visitor centers. The park also offers bike rentals, guided tours, and a free shuttle service on weekends and holidays to help visitors explore its vast expanse.

Access to the park itself is free, but some attractions charge admission fees. For instance, California Academy of Sciences tickets start at $41 for adults, while the de Young Museum charges $15 for general admission.

Discounts are available for seniors, youths, and members.

Golden Gate Park boasts a diverse array of attractions and activities suitable for all ages. Key highlights include:

California Academy of Sciences

This multifaceted museum features an aquarium, a planetarium, and a four-story rainforest.

de Young Museum

Showcasing American art from the 17th to 21st centuries, this museum also offers stunning views from its Hamon Tower.

Japanese Tea Garden

A serene spot featuring traditional Japanese landscaping, koi ponds, and a tea house.

San Francisco Botanical Garden

Home to over 8,000 plant species from around the world, this garden is perfect for nature lovers.

Conservatory of Flowers

This historic greenhouse houses a wide variety of exotic plants and flowers.

Stow Lake

A popular spot for boating and picnicking, it offers rentals of rowboats and pedal boats.

The park also hosts various annual events, such as the Hardly Strictly Bluegrass Festival and the Outside Lands Music and Arts Festival, adding to its vibrant atmosphere. Golden Gate Park is a must-visit destination in San Francisco, providing a perfect blend of nature, culture, and recreation.

The Painted Ladies

Scan the QR code to see more information from the map of The Painted Ladies

The Painted Ladies, a row of Victorian houses located along Steiner Street in San Francisco, are among the city's most iconic landmarks. These pastel-coloured homes, also known as "Postcard Row," stand proudly against the backdrop of the modern San Francisco skyline, offering a striking contrast between the historic and the contemporary. Featured prominently in the opening credits of the TV show "Full House," these houses have become a must-see attraction for visitors.

The Painted Ladies are situated at 710–720 Steiner Street, directly across from Alamo Square Park. To reach them, you can take the #5 Muni bus from downtown and exit at McAllister and Pierce Streets, then walk a short distance to the park. Alternatively, hop-on, hop-off bus tours stop here, providing a convenient option for tourists.

While the Painted Ladies themselves are private residences and not open to the public, Alamo Square Park is open from 5:00 a.m. to midnight daily, allowing visitors to enjoy the view at their leisure.

Visitors are encouraged to admire the Painted Ladies from the park and the surrounding public areas. As these homes are occupied, it is important to respect the privacy of the residents by not attempting to enter the properties or engage in disruptive behaviour.

Alamo Square Park offers several amenities, including benches, picnic areas, and restrooms. There is also a playground for children and a designated dog park area. The Lady Falcon Coffee Club, a coffee truck, operates within the park, offering refreshments to visitors.

Visiting the Painted Ladies and Alamo Square Park is free. Costs might be incurred if you choose to use public transportation or participate in guided tours that include this stop as part of a broader itinerary.

At Alamo Square Park, you can expect to see the famous Painted Ladies standing in a row with the city skyline as a picturesque backdrop. This spot is popular for photography, so bring your camera to capture the iconic view. The park itself is ideal for a relaxing picnic, a casual stroll, or simply sitting and soaking in the views. The area is also a great starting point for exploring the surrounding neighbourhood, which is filled with other Victorian and Edwardian homes.

San Francisco's Chinatown

San Francisco's Chinatown is the oldest and one of the largest Chinatowns in North America, offering a unique cultural and historical experience. Established in the mid-1800s, Chinatown became a hub for Chinese immigrants, many of whom came to work on the railroads or seek fortune during the California Gold Rush. Despite challenges and changes, it has retained its vibrant identity, making it a must-visit destination in San Francisco.

Chinatown is centred around Grant Avenue and Stockton Street, with its famous entrance marked by the Dragon Gate at Grant Avenue and Bush Street. The neighbourhood is easily accessible by various means of public transportation. If you're coming from downtown, you can take the California Street cable car line or several MUNI bus routes, such as the 30-Stockton, which runs through the heart of Chinatown. The nearest BART station is Montgomery Street, from where it's a short walk to the Dragon Gate.

Chinatown itself is open to visitors 24/7, with its streets bustling with activity at all hours. Most shops and restaurants typically operate from around 10:00 a.m. to 9:00 p.m. daily. However, hours can vary, so it's a good idea to check specific businesses if you have particular places in mind to visit.

When visiting Chinatown, respect for local customs and traditions is important. This includes not taking photos inside temples without permission, being mindful of the residents' privacy, and showing respect at historical sites and religious landmarks. Chinatown is also known for its vibrant festivals, such as the Chinese New Year Parade and the Autumn Moon Festival, where traditional practices are celebrated with parades, music, and dance.

Chinatown offers a variety of services to enhance your visit. The Chinese Culture Centre and the Chinese Historical Society of America provide educational exhibits and walking tours that delve into the history and cultural significance of the area. Numerous parks and squares, such as Portsmouth Square, offer spaces for relaxation and community gatherings.

Visiting Chinatown can fit any budget. Walking through the streets and enjoying the vibrant atmosphere is free. Dining ranges from inexpensive bakeries and dim sum spots to higher-end Chinese restaurants. Souvenirs and unique items can be found at various price points in the many shops along Grant Avenue and Stockton Street.

Chinatown is a sensory delight with its bustling streets, colourful murals, and the aroma of Chinese cuisine wafting through the air. Start your visit at the Dragon Gate and explore Grant Avenue, lined with shops selling everything from souvenirs to traditional Chinese herbs. Don't miss the Golden Gate Fortune Cookie Factory on Ross Alley, where you can see fortune cookies being made and even create your own custom messages.

Visit temples like the Tin How Temple and Kong Chow Temple to experience the spiritual side of Chinatown. For history buffs, the Chinese Historical Society of America and the WWII Pacific War Memorial Hall offer deep dives into the neighbourhood's past. Art lovers can enjoy the numerous murals and galleries scattered throughout the area.

Food is a major highlight in Chinatown. From dim sum at Good Mong Kok Bakery to an upscale dining experience at China Live, there are countless culinary delights to explore. Don't forget to visit tea shops like the Red Blossom Tea Company for a traditional tea-tasting experience.

Lombard Street

Scan the QR code to see more information from the map of Lombard Street

Lombard Street, famously known as the "Crookedest Street in the World," is one of San Francisco's most iconic attractions. This unique street features a one-block section with eight sharp hairpin turns, designed in the 1920s to reduce the hill's natural steep gradient, which was deemed too dangerous for vehicles. It's located in the affluent Russian Hill neighbourhood and offers a scenic view framed by beautifully landscaped gardens and vibrant hydrangeas.

The crooked section of Lombard Street is situated between Hyde and Leavenworth Streets. To get there, you can drive, walk, or use public transportation. The Powell-Hyde cable car line stops at the top of Lombard Street, making it a convenient option for visitors. For those driving, set your GPS to 1070 Lombard Street, but be prepared for a wait, especially during peak tourist times.

Lombard Street is open 24 hours a day, seven days a week, as it is a public street. However, visiting early in the morning or late in the afternoon on weekdays is recommended to avoid heavy traffic and crowds.

When visiting Lombard Street, it's important to respect the residents who live along the street. Avoid blocking driveways, stay on sidewalks, and refrain from littering. Drivers should be cautious and maintain a slow speed to navigate the sharp turns safely. Pedestrians are advised to use the staircases on either side of the street for a safer and more enjoyable experience.

While there are no specific services directly on Lombard Street, the nearby areas of Russian Hill and North Beach offer plenty of amenities, including cafes, restaurants, and shops. Public restrooms can be found in these neighbourhoods as well.

Visiting Lombard Street is free, whether you are walking or driving. However, if you choose to take a guided tour that includes Lombard Street, costs can vary. For instance, hop-on-hop-off bus tours or guided walking tours that cover multiple attractions, including Lombard Street, range from $54 to $179 per adult.

At Lombard Street, you can expect a picturesque experience with ample photo opportunities. The view from the top offers a stunning perspective of the city, including San Francisco Bay and Coit Tower. Walking down the street allows you to appreciate the meticulous landscaping and historic homes. Driving down is a short but thrilling experience, requiring careful navigation of the tight turns.

The area also holds historical significance. For example, the house at 900 Lombard Street was featured in Alfred Hitchcock's film "Vertigo." Another notable building is the haunted Montandon House at 1000 Lombard, which adds an element of local lore to your visit.

San Francisco Museum of Modern Art (SFMOMA)

Scan the QR code to see more information from the map of San Francisco Museum of Modern Art

The San Francisco Museum of Modern Art (SFMOMA) is one of the premier destinations for contemporary and modern art in the United States. Founded in 1935, SFMOMA was the first museum on the West Coast dedicated solely to 20th-century art. Its expansive collection and cutting-edge exhibitions make it a cultural cornerstone in San Francisco. It is housed in a striking LEED Gold-certified building in the SoMa district.

SFMOMA is located at 151 Third Street, San Francisco, CA 94103. The museum is easily accessible via public transportation, with the Powell Street and Montgomery Street BART stations nearby. Multiple MUNI bus lines also stop within a block of the museum, including the 8, 14, and 30 routes. For those driving, the museum has an on-site parking garage at 147 Minna Street, open daily from 7:00 a.m. to 11:00 p.m.

The museum is open Monday to Tuesday from 10:00 a.m. to 5:00 p.m., Thursday from noon to 8:00 p.m., and Friday to Sunday from 10:00 a.m. to 5:00 p.m. It is closed on Wednesdays. The museum store and dining options generally follow these hours but may vary slightly.

Visitors should follow museum guidelines to ensure a pleasant experience for all. This includes not touching the artwork, using only pencils for note-taking, and respecting any photography restrictions. Backpacks and large bags must be checked in at the coat check. Food and drinks are not allowed in the galleries.

SFMOMA offers several services to enhance the visitor experience. These include free public tours and audio guides available at the information desk. The museum has three dining options: Cafe 5, which offers casual dining; In Situ, an upscale restaurant with a menu inspired by renowned chefs; and a coffee bar for quick bites. The museum store features a wide range of art books, prints, and unique gifts.

Admission to SFMOMA is $30 for adults, $25 for seniors, and $23 for young adults aged 19–24. Visitors 18 and under enjoy free admission. The museum also offers free admission on the first Thursday of every month for Bay Area residents, and various discounts for groups and special ticket packages are available.

Visitors can explore seven floors of extraordinary art, including over 50,000 works encompassing painting, sculpture, photography, architecture, design, and media arts. Highlights include the Doris and Donald Fisher Collection, the largest living wall in the U.S., and the Pritzker Centre for Photography, which is the largest space dedicated to photography in an American art museum. The museum frequently hosts temporary exhibitions that showcase a diverse array of contemporary artists.

SFMOMA also offers unique programmes such as the New Work series, which commissions and displays new works by emerging artists. Monthly activities include Second Sundays for Families, where children can engage in creative projects, and various special events and workshops.

A visit to SFMOMA promises not only a deep dive into modern and contemporary art but also an engaging and dynamic cultural experience in one of San Francisco's most vibrant districts.

The Exploratorium

Scan the QR code to see more information from the map of The Exploratorium

The Exploratorium, located at Pier 15 on the Embarcadero in San Francisco, is a renowned museum dedicated to the exploration of science, art, and human perception. Founded in 1969 by physicist Dr. Frank Oppenheimer, it has become a global leader in interactive learning. In 2013, the museum moved to its current expansive waterfront location, offering stunning views of San Francisco Bay and a significantly larger space to house its exhibits.

The Exploratorium is situated at Pier 15, Embarcadero at Green Street, San Francisco, CA 94111. It is easily accessible by public transportation. The MUNI F Market and E Embarcadero streetcars stop directly in front of the museum, while several MUNI bus lines and the BART Embarcadero station are within a 10-15 minute walk. There are also nearby public parking facilities for those driving.

The museum is generally open Tuesday to Sunday from 10:00 a.m. to 5:00 p.m., with extended hours on Thursdays from 6:00 p.m. to 10:00 p.m. for the adults-only "After Dark" program. The museum is closed on Mondays, except for certain holidays.

Visitors are encouraged to engage with the exhibits, but to ensure a pleasant experience for everyone, they should follow the museum's guidelines, including not bringing food and drinks into the exhibit areas and respecting the interactive nature of the exhibits by handling them with care.

The Exploratorium provides a range of services to enhance the visitor experience. These include the Seaglass Restaurant and Seismic Joint Café, which offer a variety of dining options. The museum store offers unique gifts and educational items related to the exhibits. Additionally, there are rest areas and quiet spots throughout the museum for those needing a break.

Admission is $39.95 for adults, $29.95 for youths (ages 4–17), and $29.95 for seniors, teachers, and people with disabilities. Children aged 3 and under enter for free.

Discounted rates are available for members and San Francisco residents. For an enhanced experience, the "After Dark" programme tickets are $22.95 for general admission and $17.95 for members.

The Exploratorium features over 650 hands-on exhibits across six galleries. Visitors can explore a wide range of scientific phenomena, from biology and environmental science to human perception and the physical sciences. Highlights include the Tactile Dome, where visitors navigate through a pitch-black environment using their sense of touch, and the Fog Bridge, an outdoor installation that creates a dynamic fog experience. The museum also regularly updates its exhibits and offers unique temporary installations, ensuring there's always something new to discover.

For adults, the "After Dark" programme on Thursday evenings provides a unique opportunity to explore the museum in a more relaxed, social setting, often featuring special themes and guest speakers. Additionally, the museum hosts various educational programmes and workshops, making it a great resource for teachers and students alike.

The Exploratorium is a must-visit for anyone in San Francisco, offering a fun, educational, and interactive experience that appeals to visitors of all ages.

The Presidio

The Presidio of San Francisco is a unique blend of natural beauty, historical significance, and recreational opportunities, making it a top attraction in the city. Originally established as a military fort in 1776, the Presidio has evolved into a vibrant national park, offering a range of activities for visitors.

The Presidio is located at the northern tip of San Francisco, adjacent to the Golden Gate Bridge. The main visitor centre can be found at 210 Lincoln Boulevard. Getting to the Presidio is convenient, with several options. The free Presidio GO Shuttle provides routes from downtown San Francisco and within the park itself. Public transportation options include MUNI bus lines 28, 30, 43, and 45, which stop near various entrances to the park. For those driving, ample paid parking is available throughout the park.

The park is open daily from 6:00 a.m. to 10:00 p.m. The Presidio Visitor Centre, a great starting point for any visit, is open from 10:00 a.m. to 5:00 p.m. every day except Thanksgiving, Christmas, and New Year's Day.

Visitors are encouraged to respect the natural and historical features of the presidio. This includes staying on designated paths, not disturbing wildlife, and respecting any posted signs or guidelines, especially around historical buildings and sensitive habitats.

The Presidio offers a variety of services to enhance your visit. The Visitor Centre provides maps, information, and exhibits detailing the park's history and attractions. The park features numerous restrooms, picnic areas, and playgrounds, as well as the Presidio Tunnel Tops, a new park area with scenic overlooks, trails, and family-friendly activities. Dining options include several food trucks at the Tunnel Tops and restaurants such as the Presidio Social Club and Il Parco.

Access to the park and many of its attractions is free. However, some activities, such as guided tours or special events, may have associated costs. Parking fees range from $2.50 to $3.50 per hour, depending on the location within the park.

Visitors to the presidio can expect a wide range of activities. Outdoor enthusiasts can explore over 24 miles of hiking and biking trails, including paths that offer breathtaking views of the Golden Gate Bridge and the Pacific Ocean. History buffs will enjoy exploring landmarks such as Fort Point, a Civil War-era fort located beneath the Golden Gate Bridge, and the Officers' Club, which houses exhibits on the Presidio's military past.

The Presidio also hosts numerous events throughout the year, including outdoor concerts, ranger-led campfire talks, and volunteer opportunities like habitat restoration projects. For families, the park offers playgrounds, the Field Station with hands-on nature activities, and the new Outpost play area at Tunnel Tops.

The Presidio is a diverse and dynamic destination, offering something for everyone. It provides a rich and rewarding experience.

Coit Tower

Coit Tower, a beloved San Francisco landmark, stands 210 feet tall atop Telegraph Hill, offering panoramic views of the city and its surrounding bay. Constructed in 1933, the tower was funded by a bequest from Lillie Hitchcock Coit, a colourful patron of the city's firefighters, to beautify San Francisco. Its simple, fluted Art Deco design by architect Henry Howard makes it a distinctive feature of the city's skyline.

Scan the QR code to see more information from the map of Coit Tower

Coit Tower is located at 1 Telegraph Hill Boulevard, San Francisco, CA 94133. It's accessible by various means of transportation. The MUNI #39 Coit bus travels between Coit Tower and Fisherman's Wharf, providing a direct route. For those preferring a scenic hike, you can climb the Filbert Street stairs or the Greenwich Street stairs, both of which offer beautiful garden views and a workout on your way up the hill. Parking near the tower is limited and often busy, so public transportation or walking is recommended.

The tower is open daily from 10:00 a.m. to 6:00 p.m. from April to October and from 10:00 a.m. to 5:00 p.m. from November to March. These hours include access to the observation deck, gift shop, and café.

While visiting Coit Tower, be mindful of the historic murals on the ground floor and second floor. Touching the murals or leaning on them is prohibited to preserve their condition. Photography is allowed, but tripods and large equipment are generally not permitted. Food and drinks are not allowed inside the tower, but there is a café nearby for refreshments.

Coit Tower features several services to enhance your visit. There is a gift shop on the ground floor offering San Francisco-themed souvenirs. A café near the parking lot serves hot and cold drinks, pastries, paninis, and more. The tower also provides restrooms for visitors.

Visiting the ground floor of Coit Tower, where you can view the murals, is free. To access the observation deck, tickets cost $10 for non-resident adults, $7 for seniors and youth, and $3 for children aged 5–11. San Francisco residents enjoy discounted rates. Tickets can be purchased on-site.

At Coit Tower, visitors can explore Depression-era murals painted by local artists, which depict various aspects of 1930s California life. These murals are significant examples of the Public Works of Art Project, a New Deal program. The highlight of the visit is the observation deck, accessible via elevator or a climb up 250 stairs, which offers 360-degree views of San Francisco, including landmarks such as the Golden Gate Bridge, Alcatraz, and Lombard Street. The observation deck provides a perfect vantage point for photography, though visitors should be prepared for possible glare from the glass windows.

Coit Tower is a must-visit for its historical significance, stunning art, and unbeatable views of San Francisco.

San Francisco's top attractions encapsulate the city's rich history, vibrant culture, and stunning landscapes. Each landmark offers a unique glimpse into the diverse fabric of the city. Visitors are sure to find engaging experiences that leave lasting memories.

CHAPTER 6

Hidden Gems

San Francisco is renowned for its iconic landmarks and bustling tourist spots, but it also holds a wealth of hidden gems that offer unique and authentic experiences. These lesser-known attractions capture the essence of the city's vibrant culture, rich history, and stunning natural beauty. Discovering these hidden treasures allows you to see a different side of San Francisco, one that is filled with charming surprises and memorable adventures.

Mission District Murals

The Mission District Murals are a vibrant and colourful testament to San Francisco's rich cultural and artistic heritage. Nestled in one of the city's oldest neighbourhoods, these murals transform the streets and alleys into an open-air gallery, celebrating community, history, and activism. The murals began to appear in the 1970s as a form of expression and resistance among local artists, and today, they cover walls, garages, and storefronts, offering a dynamic and ever-evolving visual experience.

The Mission District is located in the heart of San Francisco, with the highest concentration of murals found on Balmy Alley and Clarion Alley. To get there, you can take the BART to the 24th Street Mission Station or the 16th Street Mission Station. Several

MUNI bus lines, including the 14 and 49, also service the area.

Since the murals are on public streets, they are accessible 24/7. However, for the best experience and safety, it's advisable to visit during daylight hours. This will allow you to fully appreciate the details and colours of the artwork.

While enjoying the murals, it's important to respect the neighbourhood and the residents. Avoid touching the murals, and be mindful of your surroundings. Photography is allowed, but it's courteous to ask permission if you are photographing people or private property.

The Mission District offers a variety of amenities, including numerous cafes, restaurants, and shops where you can take a break and enjoy local cuisine. There are also public restrooms in nearby parks like Mission Dolores Park.

Viewing the murals is completely free, making it an accessible and budget-friendly activity. Guided tours are available for those interested in a deeper understanding of the history and significance of the murals. These tours typically range from $15 to $25 per person and can be booked through various local tour companies.

When visiting the Mission District Murals, you can expect a rich tapestry of art that reflects the diverse cultures and histories of the community. The murals cover a wide range of themes, from social justice and political activism to cultural pride and community stories. Balmy Alley is particularly famous for its concentration of murals that focus on human rights and political struggles in Latin America, while Clarion Alley showcases a mix of contemporary art and social commentary.

In addition to viewing the murals, you can explore the lively Mission District, known for its eclectic mix of Latin American culture, hipster vibe, and historic significance. Enjoy authentic Mexican food at local taquerias, browse through unique shops, or relax in one of the district's parks.

Wave Organ

Scan the QR code to see more information from the map of Wave Organ

The Wave Organ is an enchanting acoustic sculpture located on a jetty in the Marina District of San Francisco, overlooking the Golden Gate Bridge. This unique instrument, designed by Peter Richards and built with the help of stonemason George Gonzales, harnesses the power of the ocean to create soothing, otherworldly sounds. Constructed in 1986, the Wave Organ uses a series of PVC and concrete pipes of varying lengths and diameters that interact with the movement of the waves, producing musical tones that can be heard at different points along the structure.

The Wave Organ is situated at 83 Marina Green Drive, San Francisco, CA 94123, near the tip of the jetty at the end of Yacht Road. To reach the Wave Organ, you can drive and park at the nearby Marina Green parking lot, or take public transportation with MUNI lines 30 and 43, which stop close to the Marina District. From there, it's a pleasant walk along the waterfront.

As the Wave Organ is an outdoor installation, it is accessible 24 hours a day, seven days a week. However, the best time to visit is during high tide, when the waves are more active, making the sounds produced by the organ more pronounced and varied.

Visitors are encouraged to enjoy the Wave Organ peacefully, listening to the sounds and taking in the serene environment. It is important to respect the sculpture and the surrounding area by not climbing on the pipes or damaging any part of the installation. Additionally, while the area is generally safe, visiting during daylight hours is recommended for the best experience and safety.

There are no specific services or facilities at the Wave Organ itself. However, the nearby Marina Green and Crissy Field offer restrooms, picnic areas, and plenty of open space for relaxation and recreation. Various cafes and restaurants in the Marina District provide dining options before or after your visit.

Visiting the Wave Organ is completely free, making it an ideal activity for budget-conscious travelers. The only costs you might incur are transportation and any refreshments you choose to enjoy in the area.

Upon arrival, you'll find a stone platform adorned with various listening tubes. The best way to experience the Wave Organ is to sit or kneel near the pipes and listen closely as the ocean's waves create a symphony of sounds. The experience can be both meditative and mesmerising, providing a unique way to connect with the natural rhythms of the sea.

The location also offers stunning views of the Golden Gate Bridge, Alcatraz Island, and the San Francisco skyline. It's a perfect spot for photography, a leisurely walk, or simply sitting and watching the boats sail by.

Sutro Baths

Scan the QR code to see more information from the map of Sutro Baths

The Sutro Baths, once a magnificent public swimming facility, now stand as a hauntingly beautiful ruin on the western edge of San Francisco, near the Pacific Ocean. Built in 1896 by wealthy entrepreneur Adolph Sutro, the baths were an engineering marvel of their time, featuring six saltwater pools, a massive glass enclosure, and an array of amenities, including slides, trapezes, and springboards. Despite its grandeur, the facility struggled financially and eventually closed in 1966. A fire later that year destroyed much of the remaining structure, leaving behind the atmospheric ruins that visitors explore today.

The Sutro Baths are located at the end of Point Lobos Avenue, near the intersection with 48th Avenue, San Francisco, CA 94121. Public transportation options include the MUNI bus lines 38 and 18, which stop nearby. If driving, there is a parking lot at the Lands End Visitor Centre, providing convenient access to the site.

The Sutro Baths ruins are accessible to the public daily from 6:00 a.m. to 9:30 p.m. The nearby Lands End Lookout Visitor Centre operates from 9:00 a.m. to 5:00 p.m., offering additional information and amenities for visitors.

Visitors to the Sutro Baths are encouraged to respect the historical site by staying on marked paths and not climbing on the ruins, which can be dangerous. It's important to leave no trace and preserve the natural beauty and historical significance of the area. Swimming is not allowed due to hazardous conditions, and caution should be taken near the water's edge.

The Lands End Lookout Visitor Centre provides restrooms, a gift shop, and information about the history and ecology of the area. There are also several hiking trails that start near the baths, offering scenic views and opportunities for outdoor recreation.

Visiting the Sutro Baths is free, making it an excellent option for budget-conscious travelers. The only costs you may incur are related to parking or purchasing items from the visitor centre.

At the Sutro Baths, you can expect to explore the fascinating remnants of what was once the largest indoor swimming complex in the world. The site offers a unique blend of natural beauty and historical intrigue, with waves crashing against the rocky shoreline and the ruins providing a stark contrast to the rugged landscape.

Visitors can walk along the paths and trails that weave through the ruins, discovering old staircases, tunnels, and foundations. It's a popular spot for photography, with the dramatic scenery providing a perfect backdrop. The area is also rich in wildlife, and you might spot seabirds or marine life along the shore.

Nearby, the Lands End Trail offers stunning coastal views, winding through cypress groves and leading to vantage points like Eagle's Point and Mile Rock Beach. This trail is relatively easy and suitable for most fitness levels, making it a great addition to your visit.

Lands End

Scan the QR code to see more information from the map of Lands End

Lands End is a breathtaking coastal park located at the northwestern corner of San Francisco, offering stunning ocean views, rugged cliffs, and a rich history. Part of the Golden Gate National Recreation Area, Lands End is known for its scenic beauty and trails that provide a tranquil escape from the urban hustle. The park features a combination of natural landscapes and historic landmarks, including remnants of shipwrecks and the historic Sutro Baths.

Lands End is located at 680 Point Lobos Avenue, San Francisco, CA 94121. The park is easily accessible by public transportation, with the MUNI bus lines 38 and 18 stopping nearby. If driving, there is a parking lot at the Lands End Lookout Visitor Centre, which serves as a convenient starting point for exploring the area.

Lands End is open daily from 6:00 a.m. to 9:30 p.m. The Lands End Lookout Visitor Centre is open from 9:00 a.m. to 5:00 p.m., offering additional resources and amenities for visitors.

Visitors to Lands End should stay on designated trails to protect the delicate coastal environment and for personal safety. Pets are welcome but must be kept on a leash. It's important to respect wildlife and other visitors by maintaining a clean and quiet environment.

The Lands End Lookout Visitor Centre provides restrooms, a gift shop, and exhibits detailing the natural and historical significance of the area. The visitor centre also offers maps and information on the various trails and attractions within Lands End.

Access to Lands End is free, making it a great option for budget-conscious travelers. The only expenses you might incur are for parking or purchases at the visitor centre.

At Lands End, you can expect a variety of outdoor activities and stunning vistas. The main attraction is the Lands End Trail, a well-maintained path that winds along the cliffs, offering panoramic views of the Pacific

Ocean, the Golden Gate Bridge, and the Marin Headlands. The trail is about 3.4 miles round-trip and is suitable for hikers of all levels. Along the way, you'll encounter lookout points such as Eagle's Point and Mile Rock Beach, both of which offer spectacular photo opportunities.

Lands End is also home to several historical sites. You can explore the ruins of the Sutro Baths, a former grand public swimming complex, and visit the USS San Francisco Memorial, dedicated to the famous World War II cruiser. The park also features several shipwrecks visible at low tide, adding a touch of intrigue to your visit.

The natural beauty of Lands End is complemented by its diverse wildlife. Birdwatchers can spot various seabirds, and marine mammals such as seals and whales can often be seen offshore. The area's rich flora includes coastal scrub and wildflowers, which add colour to the landscape.

Lands End offers a serene and picturesque retreat with plenty of opportunities for hiking, photography, and historical exploration.

Filbert Steps

Scan the QR code to see more information from the map of Filbert Steps

The Filbert Steps are a hidden gem in San Francisco, offering a scenic and historical pathway through lush gardens and quaint cottages as they ascend the eastern slope of Telegraph Hill. These steps are a favourite for their picturesque views and peaceful ambiance, providing a unique perspective of the city away from the usual tourist routes.

The Filbert Steps begin at the intersection of Sansome Street and Filbert Street and continue up to Coit Tower at the top of Telegraph Hill. To get there, you can take the MUNI bus lines 10, 12, or 41 to the nearby stops, or the Powell-Mason cable car, which stops a few blocks away. If driving, be aware that parking can be limited, especially near the top of Coit Tower.

The Filbert Steps are accessible 24/7 as they are a public thoroughfare. However, it is best to visit during daylight hours to fully appreciate the gardens and the views and for safety reasons.

Visitors should respect the residents living along the steps by keeping noise to a minimum and not trespassing on private property. As with any public space, it is important to keep the area clean by disposing of trash properly.

While there are no services directly on the Filbert Steps, the surrounding areas, including North Beach and the Embarcadero, offer a variety of cafes, restaurants, and shops. Coit Tower at the top of the hill provides restrooms, a gift shop, and stunning views of the city and bay.

Exploring the Filbert Steps is completely free. The only costs you might incur are related to transportation or any refreshments you choose to enjoy in the nearby neighbourhoods.

Climbing the Filbert Steps is a rewarding experience, with each section offering something unique. The lower part of the steps runs through the Grace Marchant Garden, a beautiful and meticulously maintained public garden filled with colourful flowers, native plants, and shaded areas. As you ascend, you will pass by charming historic cottages and be treated to panoramic views of San Francisco Bay, the Bay Bridge, and beyond.

The steps are steep and can be physically demanding, so wearing comfortable shoes is advisable. Along the way, you might encounter local wildlife, including the famous parrots of Telegraph Hill, adding to the steps' charm.

At the top of the Filbert Steps, you can visit Coit Tower, which features impressive murals and an observation deck offering 360-degree views of San Francisco. The climb to Coit Tower provides a sense of accomplishment and a chance to enjoy one of the city's best vantage points.

The Filbert Steps offer a blend of natural beauty, historical interest, and exercise, making them a must-visit hidden gem in San Francisco.

Baker Beach

Scan the QR code to see more information from the map of Baker Beach

Baker Beach is a stunning coastal haven located on the western edge of San Francisco, offering spectacular views of the Golden Gate Bridge, the Marin Headlands, and the Pacific Ocean. Known for its rugged cliffs and sandy shores, Baker Beach is a favourite among locals for its natural beauty, serene atmosphere, and recreational opportunities. This hidden gem provides a perfect escape from the city's hustle and bustle, allowing visitors to relax and enjoy the scenic surroundings.

Baker Beach is situated at the westernmost end of the Presidio, along Gibson Road, San Francisco, CA 94129. It is accessible by car, with a parking lot available at the end of Battery Chamberlin Road. Public transportation options include MUNI bus lines 29, 38, and 41, which stop nearby, providing convenient access to the beach.

The beach is open daily from 6:00 a.m. to 10:00 p.m., allowing visitors to enjoy the tranquil environment throughout the day. Early morning visits offer a chance to experience the beach in a quieter, more serene setting, while sunsets provide a breathtaking backdrop for an evening stroll.

Visitors to Baker Beach should respect the natural environment and follow the posted regulations. Fires and barbecues are not allowed on the beach, and pets must be kept on a leash. The northern part of Baker Beach is clothing-optional, which visitors should be aware of and respect. Additionally, swimming is not recommended due to strong currents and cold water temperatures.

Baker Beach offers several amenities to enhance your visit, including restrooms, picnic areas with tables and grills, and designated parking areas. The beach is also equipped with trash bins and recycling containers to help maintain its cleanliness. Lifeguards are not typically on duty, so visitors should exercise caution when near the water.

Visiting Baker Beach is free, making it an ideal destination for budget-conscious travelers. The only potential expenses might be transportation or any food and beverages you bring along or purchase from nearby vendors.

At Baker Beach, you can expect stunning views of the Golden Gate Bridge, particularly from the northern end of the beach. The sandy shore is perfect for sunbathing, picnicking, and beachcombing. The beach's scenic cliffs and natural beauty make it a popular spot for photography, especially during sunset when the sky is painted with vibrant colours.

For outdoor enthusiasts, the nearby Battery Chamberlin, a historic military fortification, is worth exploring. It houses a unique six-inch "disappearing gun" and offers a glimpse into the area's military history. Additionally, the Coastal Trail runs parallel to the beach, providing excellent opportunities for hiking and wildlife viewing.

Baker Beach is also a great spot for fishing, with ample space along the shoreline to cast a line. While swimming is not advised due to the strong currents, the beach provides a relaxing environment for wading and enjoying the ocean breeze.

San Francisco's hidden gems offer a rich and diverse array of experiences that showcase the city's unique charm and character. These lesser-known spots provide a deeper connection to the local culture and natural beauty, often away from the usual tourist trails. Exploring these hidden treasures reveals a side of San Francisco that is both enchanting and rewarding, adding a unique dimension to any visit.

CHAPTER 7

Activities for Different Travellers

Activities for Solo Travelers

San Francisco is an excellent destination for solo travellers, offering a myriad of activities that cater to diverse interests.

One of the best activities for solo travellers is exploring the city's vibrant neighbourhoods on foot. Start with a walking tour of the Mission District, known for its colourful murals and eclectic mix of shops and cafes. You can join a guided tour to learn about the history and significance of the area's street art, or simply wander the streets at your own pace. The Mission District is easily accessible by BART, with the 16th Street Mission Station being the closest stop.

For those who enjoy history and architecture, a visit to the historic Alcatraz Island is a must. Located in San Francisco Bay, Alcatraz was once a federal prison and is now a popular national park. You can take a ferry from Pier 33, with frequent departures throughout the day. The self-guided audio tour provides fascinating insights into the lives of the prisoners and guards who once inhabited the island. Tickets should be booked in advance, and they cost around $40 for adults.

Art lovers should not miss the San Francisco Museum of Modern Art (SFMOMA), located at 151 Third Street. The museum features an extensive collection of contemporary and modern art, including works by artists such as Andy Warhol, Jackson Pollock, and Frida Kahlo. SFMOMA is open daily, except Wednesdays, from 10:00 a.m. to 5:00 p.m., with extended hours on Thursdays. General admission is $25, and tickets can be purchased online or at the museum.

If you prefer outdoor activities, the Lands End Trail offers stunning views of the Pacific Ocean and the Golden Gate Bridge. This scenic trail is part of the Golden Gate National Recreation Area and is accessible via public transportation, with several MUNI bus lines serving the area. The trail is open daily from sunrise to sunset and is free to access. It's an excellent spot for hiking, photography, and birdwatching.

Another great option for solo travellers is exploring the Ferry Building Marketplace, located at the Embarcadero at the foot of Market Street. This historic building houses a variety of artisan food vendors, shops, and restaurants. The marketplace is open daily from 10:00 a.m. to 6:00 p.m., with extended hours on Tuesdays, Thursdays, and Saturdays for the popular farmers market. It's a perfect place to sample local delicacies and pick up unique souvenirs.

For a unique cultural experience, consider attending a performance at the San Francisco Symphony, located at Davies Symphony Hall, 201 Van Ness Avenue. The symphony offers a diverse programme of classical and contemporary music, with performances scheduled throughout the year. Tickets range from $20 to $150, depending on the performance and seating.

San Francisco offers a wealth of activities that are perfect for solo travelers. With its welcoming atmosphere and diverse attractions, San Francisco is a top destination for solo adventurers.

Activities for Couples

San Francisco is a city of romance, with its picturesque landscapes, charming neighbourhoods, and myriad activities perfect for couples seeking to create lasting memories.

One of the most romantic activities for couples is a sunset cruise on San Francisco Bay. Several companies offer these cruises, providing breathtaking views of the city skyline, the Golden Gate Bridge, and Alcatraz Island as the sun sets. Red and White Fleet and Hornblower Cruises are popular options, with departures from Pier 43 at Fisherman's Wharf. Cruises typically last 1.5 to 2 hours, and prices range from $60 to $90 per person. This intimate setting allows couples to enjoy a glass of champagne while watching the sun dip below the horizon.

For wine enthusiasts, a day trip to Napa Valley or Sonoma is a must. These renowned wine regions are just an hour's drive from San Francisco and offer romantic vineyard tours, wine tastings, and gourmet dining experiences. Many tour companies provide transportation and guided tours, such as Platypus Wine Tours and the Napa Valley Wine Train. Prices vary depending on the tour, but expect to spend around $150 to $300 per person for a full day of wine tasting and dining.

Golden Gate Park is another ideal location for a romantic outing. Couples can rent a paddleboat at Stow Lake, located in the park's western section at 50 Stow Lake Drive. Paddleboat rentals are available from 10:00 a.m. to 4:00 p.m. daily, with prices starting at $27 per hour. After a leisurely boat ride, visit the nearby Japanese Tea Garden, a tranquil spot perfect for a peaceful stroll and enjoying a cup of tea. The garden is open daily from 9:00 a.m. to 6:00 p.m., and admission is $12 for adults.

A visit to the Palace of Fine Arts offers a romantic setting for a leisurely walk. Located at 3601 Lyon Street, this architectural masterpiece is surrounded by a serene lagoon and lush greenery. It's open daily from 6:00 a.m. to 9:00 p.m., and entrance is free. Couples can enjoy the scenic beauty, take memorable photos, and perhaps even enjoy a picnic.

Dining at a rooftop restaurant with panoramic views of the city is another romantic option. Top of the Mark, located at the InterContinental Mark Hopkins at 999 California Street, offers spectacular views of San Francisco along with a fine dining experience. It's open from 4:00 p.m. to midnight daily, and reservations are recommended. Expect to spend around $50 to $100 per person.

For a cultural experience, consider attending a performance at the San Francisco Opera or Ballet. Both venues are located at the War Memorial Opera House, 301 Van Ness Avenue. Performances typically start at 7:30 PM, and tickets range from $30 to $300 depending on the seating and the show. Enjoying a world-class performance in this grand setting is sure to create a memorable evening.

San Francisco's many parks and scenic spots provide endless opportunities for romantic activities. Couples can find countless ways to enjoy each other's company in this beautiful city.

Family-Friendly Activities

San Francisco is an incredibly family-friendly city, offering a wide range of activities that cater to kids and adults alike. With its mix of educational attractions, outdoor adventures, and unique experiences, families are sure to find something to delight everyone.

One of the top family-friendly attractions is the California Academy of Sciences, located in Golden Gate Park at 55 Music Concourse Drive. This museum features an aquarium, a planetarium, and a natural history museum, all under one living roof. The academy is open daily from 9:30 a.m. to 5:00 p.m. Admission costs around $40 for adults, $30 for youth ages 12–17, and $28 for children ages 4–11. Expect to spend several hours exploring the interactive exhibits, watching a show in the planetarium, and observing the diverse marine life in the aquarium.

The San Francisco Zoo, situated at 1 Zoo Road near the southwestern corner of the city, is another fantastic destination for families. Open daily from 10:00 a.m. to 5:00 p.m., the zoo is home to over 2,000 exotic, endangered, and rescued animals. Admission fees are $25 for adults, $20 for seniors, and $18 for children ages 2–14. Families can enjoy a fun day out visiting the various animal exhibits, riding the Little Puffer Miniature Steam Train, and playing in the Elinor Friend Playground.

The Exploratorium, a hands-on museum of science, art, and human perception, is perfect for curious minds. Located at Pier 15 on the Embarcadero, the museum is open Tuesday through Sunday from 10:00 a.m. to 5:00 p.m. Admission costs are $39.95 for adults, $29.95 for youth ages 13–17, and $24.95 for children ages 4–12. The Exploratorium offers hundreds of interactive exhibits that encourage kids and adults to explore and experiment, making it both educational and entertaining.

A visit to Pier 39 in Fisherman's Wharf is a must for families. This lively waterfront area offers a variety of attractions, including the Aquarium of the Bay, the famous sea lions lounging on the docks, and the historic carousel. Pier 39 is open daily from 10:00 a.m. to 10:00 p.m. While entry to the pier is free, individual attractions like the aquarium have their own admission fees, with prices around $30 for adults and $20 for children. Families can also enjoy street performers, shops, and dining options.

Golden Gate Park itself is a treasure trove of family activities. In addition to the California Academy of Sciences, the park offers the Koret Children's Quarter playground, the carousel, and the Japanese Tea Garden. The park is open daily from 5:00 a.m. to midnight, and while entry to the park is free, some attractions within the park may charge admission fees. It's an ideal place for picnicking, biking, and enjoying outdoor activities.

A ride on one of San Francisco's historic cable cars provides a fun and unique experience for the whole family. The Powell-Hyde and Powell-Mason lines are particularly scenic, offering views of the bay and city landmarks. Cable cars operate daily from 6:00 a.m. to 12:30 a.m., with a one-way ticket costing $8 per person. Riding the cable cars not only offers a convenient way to see the city but also provides a memorable adventure.

San Francisco's family-friendly activities ensure that there is always something exciting to explore and enjoy. Families will find numerous ways to create lasting memories in this vibrant city.

CHAPTER 8

Outdoor Activities

Hiking Trails

San Francisco is renowned for its stunning natural beauty, and one of the best ways to experience this is by exploring its numerous hiking trails. The city's trails offer a variety of experiences, each with its own unique scenery and challenges.

Lands End

One of the most popular hiking destinations in San Francisco is Lands End. Located at 680 Point Lobos Avenue, this trail offers breathtaking views of the Pacific Ocean, the Golden Gate Bridge, and the rugged coastline. The main Lands End Trail is a 3.4-mile round trip that is accessible to hikers of all levels. To get there, you can take the MUNI bus lines 38 or 18, which stop near the entrance. The trail is open daily from sunrise to sunset, and admission is free. As you hike, you can explore historic sites like the Sutro Baths ruins and the USS San Francisco Memorial. The trail is well-maintained with clear signage, and there are benches and rest areas along the way. Dogs are allowed on a leash, and it's important to stay on marked paths to protect the environment and ensure safety.

Presidio

Another excellent hiking location is the Presidio, a historic park that offers several scenic trails. The Presidio is located at 210 Lincoln Boulevard, and it's easily accessible by the free PresidiGo Shuttle from downtown San Francisco or by various MUNI bus lines. The park is open daily from 6:00 a.m. to 10:00 p.m. One of the most popular trails is the Presidio Promenade, a 2.1-mile trail that provides panoramic views of the Golden Gate Bridge and San Francisco Bay. Along the way, hikers can visit landmarks such as Fort Point and the Main Post. The park offers various amenities, including restrooms, picnic areas, and visitor centers. Entry to the park is free, and it provides a peaceful escape with a mix of natural and historical sights.

Mount Sutro

For those looking for a more challenging hike, Mount Sutro is an excellent choice. Located at the UCSF Medical Centre, Mount Sutro Open Space Reserve offers a network of trails through a dense eucalyptus forest. The trails are open daily from 6:00 a.m. to 6:00 p.m., and admission is free. The Historic Trail and the Fairy Gates Trail are popular routes, offering moderate to strenuous hikes with elevation changes and beautiful views. The trails can be accessed by public transportation, with the N-Judah MUNI light rail stopping nearby. Hikers should be prepared for varying weather conditions and bring water and snacks, as services are limited within the reserve.

Glen Canyon Park

Another hidden gem is Glen Canyon Park, located at Elk Street and Chenery Street. This 70-acre park features a variety of trails that wind through a dramatic canyon, offering a unique natural retreat within the city. The park is open daily from 5:00 a.m. to midnight, and admission is free. To get there, you can take the MUNI bus lines 44 or 52. The trails vary in difficulty, making them suitable for all ages and fitness levels. The park also features playgrounds, picnic areas, and tennis courts, providing additional recreational opportunities.

The Twin Peaks Trail

The Twin Peaks trail also offers one of the best vantage points in San Francisco. Located at the intersection of Twin Peaks Boulevard and Christmas Tree Point Road, this trail provides a short but steep hike to the top of the city's second-highest peak. The trail is accessible by car, with parking available at the top, or by public transportation via the 37-Corbett MUNI bus line. The trail is open 24/7, and there is no admission fee. From the summit, hikers are rewarded with 360-degree views of the city, the bay, and beyond. It's a perfect spot for photography, especially at sunrise or sunset.

Beaches

San Francisco's beaches offer a blend of stunning natural beauty and vibrant city life, making them perfect destinations for outdoor enthusiasts. Each beach has its own unique charm, from panoramic views of the Golden Gate Bridge to opportunities for surfing and beachcombing. Here's a detailed guide to some of the best beaches in San Francisco:.

Baker Beach

Baker Beach is one of the most picturesque beaches in San Francisco, offering stunning views of the Golden Gate Bridge and the Marin Headlands. Located at the western edge of the Presidio, the beach is accessible via Lincoln Boulevard and Bowley Street. You can get there by car, with parking available at the lot at the end of Bowley Street, or by taking the MUNI bus lines 29 and 38. Baker Beach is open daily from 6:00 a.m. to 10:00 p.m. Visitors should be aware that the northern part of the beach is clothing-optional. The beach is a popular spot for picnicking, fishing, and taking in the breathtaking views. While swimming is not recommended due to strong currents and cold water, the beach is perfect for a relaxing day by the ocean.

Ocean Beach

Ocean Beach is the longest beach in San Francisco, stretching along the western edge of the city for about 3.5 miles. It's located adjacent to the Great Highway and is easily accessible by car, with ample parking available along the highway and at nearby lots. Public transportation options include the N-Judah MUNI light rail and several bus lines, such as the 5, 31, and 38. Ocean Beach is open daily from 6:00 a.m. to 10:00 p.m. This beach is known for its strong waves and is a favourite spot for surfers, although the water is cold and the currents are strong, so it's not ideal for casual swimming. The beach offers fire pits for bonfires, which are especially popular during the cooler months. Nearby, you'll find the Beach Chalet Brewery & Restaurant, which offers food, drinks, and restrooms.

China Beach

China Beach is a small, secluded beach located in the Sea Cliff neighbourhood, offering a quieter and more intimate experience. The beach is at 490 Sea Cliff Avenue and is accessible by car, with limited parking available. Public transportation options include the 1-California and 38-Geary MUNI bus lines. China Beach is open daily from 6:00 a.m. to 10:00 p.m. This beach offers beautiful views of the Golden Gate Bridge and is a great spot for picnics and beachcombing. There are restrooms, showers, and picnic tables available, making it a convenient spot for a relaxing day out. The beach is known for its calm atmosphere and scenic beauty, making it perfect for families and those seeking a peaceful retreat.

Crissy Field

Crissy Field is another popular beach, part of the larger Crissy Field recreation area within the Presidio. It's located along Mason Street and is easily accessible by car, with parking available at East Beach and West Bluff. Public transportation options include the 30-Stockton and 43-Masonic MUNI bus lines. Crissy Field is open daily from 6:00 a.m. to 10:00 p.m. This beach offers stunning views of the Golden Gate Bridge, Alcatraz Island, and the San Francisco skyline. It's a great spot for walking, jogging, picnicking, and windsurfing. The area also features a café, restrooms, and picnic areas. The Crissy Field Centre offers educational programmes and activities, making it a perfect destination for families.

Marshall's Beach

Marshall's Beach is a hidden gem located just south of Baker Beach, offering some of the most spectacular views of the Golden Gate Bridge. The beach is accessible via a steep trail from the parking lot at the end of Langdon Court, near Battery Godfrey. It's a bit more secluded and less crowded than other beaches, making it a great spot for photography and enjoying the natural beauty in solitude. The beach is open daily from sunrise to sunset. There are no facilities or services at Marshall's Beach, so visitors should come prepared with their supplies.

Parks and Gardens

San Francisco's parks and gardens offer a lush retreat from the urban hustle, providing spaces for relaxation, recreation, and exploration. These green havens are scattered throughout the city, each offering its own unique charm and attractions.

Golden Gate Park

Golden Gate Park is undoubtedly the crown jewel of San Francisco's parks. Spanning over 1,017 acres, it is home to a variety of attractions, including the California Academy of Sciences, the de Young Museum, the Japanese Tea Garden, and the San Francisco Botanical Garden. Located at 501 Stanyan Street, the park is easily accessible by public transportation, with several MUNI lines such as the 5, 7, 21, and N-Judah light rail serving the area. The park is open daily from 5:00 a.m. to midnight. Entry to the park is free, but some attractions within it have their own admission fees. Visitors can enjoy a wide range of activities, including hiking, biking, picnicking, and paddle boating on Stow Lake. The park also hosts numerous events and festivals throughout the year, making it a lively destination for both locals and tourists.

Japanese Tea Garden

The Japanese Tea Garden within Golden Gate Park is the oldest public Japanese garden in the United States. Located at 75 Hagiwara Tea Garden Drive, it is a serene spot featuring traditional Japanese landscaping, koi ponds, pagodas, and a teahouse. The garden is open daily from 9:00 a.m. to 6:00 p.m. Admission fees are $10 for adults, $7 for seniors, and $3 for children aged 5–11. Free admission is available to San Francisco residents on certain days of the week. The garden provides a peaceful retreat where visitors can enjoy a cup of tea while taking in the tranquil surroundings.

San Francisco Botanical Garden

The San Francisco Botanical Garden, also within Golden Gate Park, spans 55 acres and features over 8,000 different kinds of plants from around the world. It is located at 1199 9th Avenue and is open daily from 7:30 a.m. to 7:00 p.m. during the summer and until 5:00 p.m. in the winter. Admission is $10 for adults, $7 for seniors and youth, and free for children under 4. San Francisco residents can enter for free with proof of residency. The garden offers various themed gardens, including a succulent garden, a redwood grove, and a Mediterranean garden, providing a diverse and educational experience for visitors.

Presidio

The Presidio of San Francisco, another must-visit park, is a former military base turned national park located at 210 Lincoln Boulevard. The Presidio offers a mix of natural beauty, historical sites, and recreational activities. Key attractions include Crissy Field, the Presidio Promenade, and the Main Post. The park is open daily from 6:00 a.m. to 10:00 p.m. and is accessible by the free PresidiGo Shuttle from downtown San Francisco or various MUNI bus lines. The Presidio offers hiking and biking trails, picnic areas, and educational programmes, making it a versatile destination for outdoor enthusiasts. Entry to the park is free, though some activities and events may have associated costs.

Alamo Square Park

Alamo Square Park is a picturesque park located at Steiner Street and Hayes Street, famous for its Painted Ladies, a row of colourful Victorian houses. The park is open daily from 5:00 a.m. to midnight. It features a playground, tennis courts, and plenty of green space for picnicking and relaxing. The park offers stunning views of the San Francisco skyline and is a popular spot for photography.

Buena Vista Park

Buena Vista Park, San Francisco's oldest park, located at Haight Street and Buena Vista Avenue East, offers steep trails and panoramic views of the city. The park is open daily from 5:00 a.m. to midnight. It's a great spot for hiking, with trails that wind through eucalyptus groves and up to scenic viewpoints. The park's rugged terrain and natural beauty make it a hidden gem in the heart of the city.

San Francisco's parks and gardens provide diverse outdoor experiences that offer something for everyone.

Biking Routes

San Francisco is a city perfectly suited for biking enthusiasts, offering a diverse range of routes that cater to all skill levels. From scenic waterfront paths to challenging hilly terrain, the city's biking routes provide a unique way to explore its iconic landmarks and natural beauty. Here's a detailed guide to some of the best biking routes in San Francisco.

The Embarcadero to Crissy Field

One of the most popular biking routes in San Francisco starts at the Ferry Building on the Embarcadero and follows the waterfront to Crissy Field. This flat, scenic route is perfect for cyclists of all levels and offers stunning views of the Bay Bridge, Alcatraz, and the Golden Gate Bridge. To get there, take BART or MUNI to the Embarcadero Station. The route is accessible 24/7 and is free to use. Along the way, you'll pass through Fisherman's Wharf and Fort Mason, where you can stop for refreshments or take a break to enjoy the views. The path continues through the Marina District and ends at Crissy Field, a popular spot for picnicking and enjoying the beach.

Golden Gate Park Loop

Golden Gate Park offers a network of biking trails that wind through its lush gardens, past museums, and along serene lakes. The main loop is approximately 7 miles and can be accessed from various points in the park, with entrances at Stanyan Street, Lincoln Way, and Fulton Street. Public transportation options include the N-Judah light rail and several MUNI bus lines that stop near the park. Golden Gate Park is open daily from 5:00 AM to midnight, and the trails are free to use. Cyclists can explore attractions such as the de Young Museum, the California Academy of Sciences, and the Japanese Tea Garden. The park also has designated bike lanes and plenty of spots to lock up your bike if you want to explore on foot.

The Wiggle

The Wiggle is a well-known, cyclist-friendly route that navigates the hilly terrain of San Francisco with minimal elevation gain. It starts at Market Street and Duboce Avenue and winds its way through the Lower Haight and the Panhandle before reaching Golden Gate Park. The route is marked with green bike symbols on the pavement and is accessible 24/7. To get there, take the N-Judah or any MUNI bus that stops near Market Street. The Wiggle is a favourite among locals for its gentle incline and scenic, tree-lined streets. Along the way, you'll find numerous cafes and shops where you can stop for a break.

Marin Headlands Loop

For a more challenging ride, the Marin Headlands Loop offers steep climbs and rewarding views of the Golden Gate Bridge and the Pacific Ocean. Starting at the Golden Gate Bridge, you'll cross over into Marin County and follow Conzelman Road up to Hawk Hill. The loop is about 10 miles roundtrip and includes several steep sections. To get to the starting point, you can take the 28-19th Avenue MUNI bus to the Golden Gate Bridge. The route is accessible 24/7 and is free to use. Along the way, you'll encounter breathtaking vistas and have the chance to explore historic military batteries. Be sure to bring plenty of water and wear layers, as the weather can change quickly.

The Great Highway

The Great Highway runs along the western edge of San Francisco, parallel to Ocean Beach. This flat, scenic route is ideal for a leisurely ride and offers stunning ocean views. The route starts at the intersection of Lincoln Way and Great Highway and continues south to Skyline Boulevard. There is ample parking available along the route, and public transportation options include the N-Judah light rail and several MUNI bus lines. The Great Highway is open 24/7 and is free to use. Along the way, you can stop at the Beach Chalet for a meal or continue your ride into Golden Gate Park.

San Francisco's biking routes offer a fantastic way to explore the city's diverse landscapes and iconic landmarks. From waterfront paths and park loops to challenging hills and coastal rides, the city's biking routes cater to all preferences and skill levels.

Water Sports

San Francisco offers an array of water sports that cater to both adventure seekers and those looking to enjoy the city's stunning waterfront from a different perspective. From kayaking in the bay to surfing the Pacific waves, here's a detailed guide to the best water sports activities in San Francisco.

Kayaking and Paddleboarding

One of the best places to enjoy kayaking and paddleboarding is Mission Creek, located in South Beach Harbour near AT&T Park. The address is 789 Terry A. Francois Boulevard, San Francisco, CA 94158. City Kayak offers rentals and guided tours, making it easy for both beginners and experienced paddlers to explore the bay. They are open daily from 9:00 a.m. to 6:00 p.m. Kayak rentals typically cost around $30 per hour, and guided tours start at about $65 per person. Expect to paddle past houseboats, under historic bridges, and enjoy views of the city skyline and Oracle Park.

Surfing

For surfing enthusiasts, Ocean Beach is the go-to spot. Located along the Great Highway, this 3.5-mile stretch of beach offers powerful waves suitable for intermediate and advanced surfers. The beach is accessible by car with ample parking along the Great Highway, and public transportation options include the N-Judah MUNI light rail and several bus lines. Ocean Beach is open daily from sunrise to sunset. While the waves are thrilling, the water is cold, and the currents are strong, so wetsuits are recommended, and surfers should always check local conditions and surf advisories.

Sailing

Sailing is a popular water sport in San Francisco Bay, with several companies offering rentals and lessons. Sailing SF is one such provider, located at Pier 39, San

Francisco, CA 94133. They offer a range of options, from private charters to group sailing lessons. Pier 39 is easily accessible by public transportation, including the F-Market and Wharves streetcars and various MUNI bus lines. Sailing SF operates daily, and prices for sailing experiences vary, starting around $75 per person for group lessons. Expect to sail under the Golden Gate Bridge, around Alcatraz Island, and enjoy panoramic views of the city skyline.

Windsurfing and Kiteboarding

Crissy Field is a hotspot for windsurfing and kiteboarding, thanks to its consistent winds and beautiful backdrop. Located at 1199 East Beach, San Francisco, CA 94129, Crissy Field offers ample parking and is accessible via the 30-Stockton and 43-Masonic MUNI bus lines. The beach is open daily from 6:00 a.m. to 10:00 p.m. Boardsports California offers rentals and lessons, with windsurfing rentals starting at about $50 per hour. Crissy Field is perfect for both beginners and advanced windsurfers, with shallow waters near the shore and stronger winds farther out.

Fishing

San Francisco Bay offers excellent fishing opportunities, with popular spots including Fort Point and Candlestick Point State Recreation Area. Fort Point is located at Long Avenue and Marine Drive, San Francisco, CA 94129, near the Golden Gate Bridge, and is accessible by car or the 28-19th Avenue MUNI bus line. Candlestick Point is located at 500 Hunters Point Motorway, San

Francisco, CA 94124, and is accessible by car, with parking available on-site. Both locations are open daily from sunrise to sunset. Fishing permits are required for anyone over the age of 16, and these can be purchased online or at local sporting goods stores. Expect to catch species such as striped bass, halibut, and rockfish.

Boat Rentals and Tours

Pier 39 and Fisherman's Wharf are prime locations for boat rentals and tours. The Blue & Gold Fleet at Pier 41 offers a variety of boat tours, including trips to Alcatraz Island and sightseeing cruises around the bay. The address for Pier 41 is Beach Street and The Embarcadero, San Francisco, CA 94133. Public transportation options include the F-Market and Wharves streetcars and various MUNI bus lines. Tours typically operate daily from 9:00 a.m. to 6:00 p.m., and prices range from $30 to $70 per person. Expect to see iconic sights like the Golden Gate Bridge, Alcatraz Island, and the city skyline from the water.

San Francisco's water sports offer a unique and exciting way to explore the city's waterfront and natural beauty. These activities provide a refreshing escape and an opportunity to see San Francisco from a new perspective.

CHAPTER 9

For Kids

San Francisco is a fantastic city for families with kids, offering a wide range of activities that are both fun and educational. This chapter points out some of the best kid-friendly activities in San Francisco.

California Academy of Sciences

Scan the QR code to book tickets for the California Academy of Sciences.

The California Academy of Sciences, located in Golden Gate Park, is a must-visit for families. This museum features an aquarium, a planetarium, a natural history museum, and a rainforest all under one living roof. The address is 55 Music Concourse Drive, San Francisco, CA 94118. To get there, you can take the N-Judah light rail or several MUNI bus lines that stop near the park. The museum is open daily from 9:30 AM to 5:00 PM. Admission costs around $40 for adults and $30 for children aged 3-17. Inside, kids can marvel at the living roof, explore the four-story rainforest, and watch a planetarium show. The museum also offers interactive exhibits and educational programs, making it a hit with kids and adults alike.

Exploratorium

The Exploratorium is an interactive museum of science, art, and human perception located at Pier 15 on the Embarcadero. The museum is designed to spark curiosity and encourage learning through hands-on exhibits. The address is Pier 15, The Embarcadero, San Francisco, CA 94111. It's accessible by public transportation, including the F-Market & Wharves streetcar and various MUNI bus lines. The Exploratorium is open Tuesday through Sunday from 10:00 AM to 5:00 PM. Admission costs $29.95 for adults and $19.95 for children aged 4-12. Expect to spend several hours exploring the hundreds of exhibits that cover topics like electricity, sound, and motion. There are also outdoor exhibits and a café with kid-friendly options.

San Francisco Zoo

Scan the QR code to book tickets for the San Francisco Zoo

The San Francisco Zoo, located at 1 Zoo Road near the southwestern corner of the city, is home to over 2,000 animals representing more than 250 species. The zoo offers various exhibits and educational programmes aimed at children. The zoo is open daily from 10:00 a.m. to 5:00 p.m. Admission fees are about $25 for adults, $18 for children aged 4–14, and free for kids under 3. Public transportation options include the L-Taraval light rail and the 23-Monterey and 18-46th Avenue MUNI bus lines. At the zoo, kids can enjoy the Leanne B. Roberts African Savanna, the Primate Discovery Centre, and the

Children's Zoo, which features a petting zoo and play area. The zoo also offers daily animal feedings and educational talks.

Children's Creativity Museum

The Children's Creativity Museum, located at 221 4th Street, is a hands-on multimedia arts and technology museum for kids. The museum focuses on fostering creativity through interactive exhibits and workshops. The museum is easily accessible by the Yerba Buena/Moscone Station on the T-Third Street and N-Judah light rail lines. It's open Thursday through Sunday from 10:00 a.m. to 4:00 p.m. Admission is about $15 for both adults and children. Inside, kids can engage in activities such as creating clay animation movies, designing digital art, and exploring a music studio. The museum also has an outdoor carousel and a creativity store.

Aquarium of the Bay

Located at Pier 39, the Aquarium of the Bay focuses on local marine life in San Francisco Bay. The address is The Embarcadero & Beach Street, San Francisco, CA 94133. Public transportation options include the F-Market and Wharves streetcars and several MUNI bus lines. The aquarium is open daily from 11:00 a.m. to 6:00 p.m. Admission costs around $30 for adults and $20 for children aged 4–12. Kids can walk through clear tunnels surrounded by thousands of marine animals, touch sea stars and anemones at the touch pools, and watch animal feedings and presentations. The aquarium also offers educational programmes and guided tours.

Bay Area Discovery Museum

Located just across the Golden Gate Bridge in Sausalito, the Bay Area Discovery Museum offers hands-on, interactive exhibits designed for children aged 0–10. The address is 557 McReynolds Road, Sausalito, CA 94965. To get there, you can drive or take the Golden Gate Transit bus. The museum is open Tuesday through Sunday from 9:00 a.m. to 4:00 p.m. Admission costs about $20 for adults and children. The museum features outdoor and indoor exhibits, including art studios, a science and imagination lab, and a tot spot for the youngest visitors. Special events and programmes are offered throughout the year, making it a dynamic place for children to learn and play.

Ghirardelli Square

Ghirardelli Square, located at 900 North Point Street, is a historic site that has been transformed into a lively shopping and dining area. It's easily accessible by the F-Market and Wharves streetcars and various MUNI bus lines. The square is open daily from 10:00 a.m. to 10:00 p.m. One of the main attractions for kids is the Ghirardelli Chocolate Experience, where they can watch chocolate being made and enjoy a delicious sundae. The square also hosts various family-friendly events throughout the year, such as holiday light displays and live music performances.

Tips for Kids

Dress in layers.

San Francisco's weather can be unpredictable, so it's best to dress in layers to stay comfortable throughout the day.

Stay Hydrated

Bring water bottles to keep hydrated, especially when exploring outdoor attractions.

Use Sunscreen

Even on cloudy days, it's important to use sunscreen to protect against UV rays.

Plan Ahead

Many attractions have specific hours and may require tickets, so plan ahead to make the most of your visit.

Safety First

Always keep an eye on your children, especially in crowded areas and near water.

San Francisco is brimming with activities that cater specifically to children, offering a blend of fun and educational experiences. With this, families are sure to find plenty of engaging and enriching activities to enjoy together.

CHAPTER 10

Culinary Delights and Nightlife

San Francisco's culinary scene and nightlife are a feast for the senses, offering an incredible array of experiences for every taste and interest. The city's diverse neighbourhoods each bring their own lavor. As the sun sets, the city transforms, revealing a vibrant nightlife filled with cosy bars, lively clubs, and entertainment venues that keep the energy high. This dynamic mix makes San Francisco a true haven for those seeking both culinary delights and an exciting night out.

Dishes

San Francisco's culinary scene is renowned for its diversity and innovation, but some dishes have become iconic, embodying the city's unique flavours and cultural heritage. Here are some must-try dishes.

Clam Chowder in a Sourdough Bread Bowl

A quintessential San Francisco dish is clam chowder served in a sourdough bread bowl. This hearty dish combines creamy, rich clam chowder with the tangy, crusty goodness of sourdough bread. The chowder typically includes clams, potatoes, onions, and celery, all cooked in a creamy broth. The sourdough bread, with its distinctive tang, is perfect for soaking up the chowder.

You can find this dish at many places along Fisherman's Wharf, but Boudin Bakery is one of the most famous spots. Located at 160 Jefferson Street, Boudin has been baking sourdough since 1849 and offers a fantastic version of this classic dish. The bakery is open daily from 8:00 a.m. to 9:00 p.m.

Dungeness Crab

Dungeness crab is a local delicacy that's particularly popular during the winter months, when the crabbing season is at its peak. The sweet, tender meat of the Dungeness crab can be enjoyed in various preparations, from steamed or boiled to cracked and served with butter.

Crab House at Pier 39, located at Pier 39 Concourse, is a great place to enjoy this dish. The restaurant is open daily from 11:00 a.m. to 9:00 p.m., and it offers stunning views of the bay along with its delicious crab dishes. Another excellent spot is Fisherman's Wharf, where you can find fresh crab stands and seafood restaurants offering this local treat.

Mission-Style Burrito

The Mission-style burrito, originating from the Mission District, is a large, foil-wrapped burrito filled with rice, beans, meat, salsa, and other ingredients like guacamole and sour cream. It's known for its generous size and variety of fillings.

La Taqueria, located at 2889 Mission Street, is often cited as one of the best places to get a Mission-style burrito. The restaurant is open Monday through Saturday from 11:00 a.m. to 8:00 p.m. and is famous for its carne asada and carnitas burritos. Expect a line, as this spot is a favourite among locals and tourists alike.

Cioppino

Cioppino is a hearty seafood stew that reflects San Francisco's Italian heritage. It typically includes a mix of clams, mussels, shrimp, scallops, squid, fish, and crab, all simmered in a tomato-based broth with wine and spices.

Scoma's, located at Pier 47, Al Scoma Way, is renowned for its cioppino. The restaurant is open daily from 11:30 a.m. to 9:30 p.m. and offers a cosy waterfront dining experience. Another excellent place to try cioppino is Tadich Grill at 240 California Street, one of the oldest restaurants in the city, open from Monday to Saturday, 11:00 a.m. to 9:30 p.m.

Ghirardelli Chocolate

Ghirardelli chocolate is a must-try for anyone with a sweet tooth. The Ghirardelli Chocolate Company, founded in 1852, offers a wide range of chocolate treats, from classic squares to decadent sundaes.

The Ghirardelli Ice Cream and Chocolate Shop at Ghirardelli Square, 900 North Point Street, is the best place to indulge in these sweet treats. The shop is open daily from 10:00 a.m. to 10:00 p.m. and offers a variety of chocolate-based desserts, including the famous hot fudge sundae.

Sourdough Bread

San Francisco's sourdough bread, with its distinctive tangy flavour and chewy texture, is a must-try. The unique flavour comes from the wild yeast and bacteria in the Bay Area's environment, which give the bread its characteristic taste.

Boudin Bakery, with locations including the flagship bakery at Fisherman's Wharf, is the quintessential place to experience San Francisco sourdough. Boudin offers a variety of breads and bakery items, and you can watch the bakers at work through the large windows.

Tips for Enjoying San Francisco's Culinary Scene

Arrive Early

Many popular spots, especially those at Fisherman's Wharf and the Mission District, can get crowded. Arriving early can help you avoid long lines.

Dress Comfortably

San Francisco's weather can be unpredictable. Dressing in layers will keep you comfortable, whether you're dining indoors or outdoors.

Share Dishes

Many of these iconic dishes are quite hearty. Sharing dishes with your group allows you to sample more of what the city has to offer.

Explore Neighbourhoods

Each neighbourhood has its own culinary specialties. Don't hesitate to venture beyond the tourist areas to find hidden gems.

San Francisco's iconic dishes offer a taste of the city's rich cultural history and its innovative culinary scene.

Fine Dining

San Francisco is home to some of the finest dining establishments in the country, offering a blend of innovative cuisine, impeccable service, and elegant atmospheres. Here are some of the finest dining restaurants in San Francisco:.

Restaurant Gary Danko

Restaurant Gary Danko is a Michelin-starred establishment located at 800 North Point Street, near Ghirardelli Square. Known for its refined American cuisine with French influences, this restaurant offers an exquisite dining experience. To get there, you can take the Powell-Hyde cable car or the 19-Polk MUNI bus line. Gary Danko is open daily for dinner from 5:30 p.m. to 10:00 p.m.

Website

[Restaurant Gary Danko San Francisco](#)

The menu features dishes like lobster risotto, roasted quail, and beef tenderloin, along with an extensive wine list to complement the meal. The restaurant caters to a sophisticated clientele, making it ideal for special occasions and romantic dinners. Expect to spend around $100 to $150 per person. The ambiance is elegant, and the service is impeccable, ensuring a memorable dining experience.

Benu

Benu, located at 22 Hawthorne Street in the SoMa district, is another Michelin-starred restaurant known for its contemporary Asian-inspired cuisine. To reach Benu, you can take the BART to Montgomery Street Station or the MUNI bus lines that stop nearby. Benu is open for dinner Tuesday through Saturday from 5:30 PM to 9:30 PM.

Website

[Benu](#)

Chef Corey Lee, a James Beard Award winner, presents a tasting menu that changes seasonally, featuring dishes like thousand-year-old quail egg and lobster coral xiao long bao. The restaurant offers a serene and minimalist ambiance, catering to a discerning crowd seeking a unique culinary adventure. The tasting menu is priced at approximately $325 per person, with optional wine pairings available.

Atelier Crenn

Atelier Crenn, located at 3127 Fillmore Street in the Marina District, is renowned for its poetic and artistic approach to French cuisine. To get there, you can take the 22-Fillmore or 30-Stockton MUNI bus lines. The restaurant is open for dinner Tuesday through Saturday from 5:30 p.m. to 9:30 p.m.

Website

Atelier Crenn

Chef Dominique Crenn, the first female chef in the U.S. to earn three Michelin stars, creates a narrative through her tasting menu, with each dish representing a part of her personal story and philosophy. The restaurant caters to a sophisticated and adventurous clientele. The multi-course tasting menu costs around $410 per person, with wine pairings starting at $220. The service is attentive and personalised, ensuring an intimate and unforgettable dining experience.

Quince

Quince is an elegant, three-Michelin-starred restaurant located at 470 Pacific Avenue in Jackson Square. Known for its contemporary Californian cuisine with Italian influences, Quince offers a refined dining experience. To get there, take the 1-California or 10-Townsend MUNI bus lines. The restaurant is open for dinner Tuesday through Saturday from 5:30 p.m. to 9:30 p.m.

Website

Quince Restaurant

Chef Michael Tusk crafts a seasonal tasting menu featuring ingredients sourced from the restaurant's own farm. Dishes like tortellini with black truffle and abalone with dashi are complemented by an extensive wine list. Quince caters to a sophisticated and discerning clientele, making it perfect for celebratory occasions. The tasting menu is priced at around $365 per person, with wine pairings available.

Saison

Saison, located at 178 Townsend Street in SoMa, is a renowned fine dining establishment with a focus on seasonal and wood-fired cuisine. To reach Saison, you can take the N-Judah light rail or various MUNI bus lines to the nearby stops. The restaurant is open for dinner Wednesday through Sunday from 5:30 p.m. to 9:00 p.m.

Website

Saison

Chef Joshua Skenes presents a tasting menu that highlights the finest seasonal ingredients, with dishes often prepared over an open flame. The intimate and rustic-chic atmosphere caters to a high-end clientele looking for a unique and immersive dining experience. The tasting menu is priced at approximately $398 per person, with an optional wine pairing.

Tips for Fine Dining in San Francisco

Reservations

Most fine-dining restaurants in San Francisco require reservations, often weeks or months in advance, so plan accordingly.

Dress Code

Fine dining establishments typically have a dress code, often business casual or formal. Check the restaurant's website for specific requirements.

Dietary Restrictions

If you have dietary restrictions, inform the restaurant when making your reservation to ensure they can accommodate your needs.

Timing

Arrive on time for your reservation to ensure you can enjoy the full experience, as some tasting menus are timed courses.

San Francisco's fine dining scene offers an extraordinary array of culinary experiences, each providing a unique blend of flavours, presentations, and atmospheres.

Casual Dining

San Francisco's casual dining scene is as diverse and dynamic as the city itself. From hearty burritos in the Mission District to the freshest seafood at Fisherman's Wharf, these casual eateries offer something for everyone. Here are some of the best casual dining spots that both locals and tourists love.

La Taqueria

La Taqueria, located at 2889 Mission Street, is renowned for its Mission-style burritos and tacos. This no-frills spot has become a local institution, drawing in crowds with its generous portions and delicious flavors. The restaurant is easily accessible by the 14-Mission or 49-Van Ness-Mission MUNI bus lines. La Taqueria is open daily from 11:00 AM to 8:00 PM.

Website

[La Taqueria](#)

The menu features a variety of burritos, including carne asada, carnitas, and pollo, all wrapped in fresh tortillas and packed with rice, beans, and your choice of toppings. The casual, lively atmosphere caters to a diverse crowd, from local families to tourists seeking an authentic taste of San Francisco's Mexican cuisine. Expect to spend around $10 to $15 per meal.

Tony's Pizza Napoletana

Tony's Pizza Napoletana, located at 1570 Stockton Street in North Beach, offers some of the best pizza in the city. Owned by 13-time World Pizza Champion Tony Gemignani, this pizzeria is a favorite among locals and visitors alike. To get there, you can take the 8-Bayshore or 30-Stockton MUNI bus lines. The restaurant is open Monday to Thursday from 12:00 PM to 10:00 PM, Friday from 12:00 PM to 11:00 PM, Saturday from 12:00 PM to 11:00 PM, and Sunday from 12:00 PM to 10:00 PM.

Website

Tony's Pizza Napoletana

Tony's specializes in a variety of pizza styles, including Neapolitan, New York, and Detroit. The Margherita pizza, made with San Marzano tomatoes, fresh mozzarella, and basil, is a must-try. The restaurant also offers a selection of pasta, salads, and antipasti. The family-friendly environment and extensive menu make it a great spot for group dining. Prices range from $15 to $30 per pizza.

Swan Oyster Depot

Swan Oyster Depot, located at 1517 Polk Street, is a historic seafood counter that has been serving fresh seafood since 1912. This family-owned establishment is known for its fresh oysters, clam chowder, and crab cocktails. The restaurant is accessible by the 19-Polk

MUNI bus line and is open Monday through Saturday from 10:30 AM to 5:30 PM.

The seating is limited to a counter, which adds to the charm and often results in lines out the door. Despite the wait, the casual, intimate setting and high-quality seafood make it worth the effort. Prices are reasonable, with most meals costing around $20 to $30.

Tartine Bakery

Tartine Bakery, located at 600 Guerrero Street in the Mission District, is a must-visit for anyone with a sweet tooth. This artisanal bakery is famous for its morning buns, croissants, and rustic country bread. To get there, you can take the J-Church MUNI light rail or the 14-Mission bus line. Tartine is open daily from 7:30 AM to 8:00 PM.

Website

Tartine Bakery

The bakery also serves sandwiches, coffee, and tea, making it a perfect spot for a casual breakfast or lunch. The bustling, cozy atmosphere attracts a mix of locals and tourists. While seating is limited, many patrons enjoy taking their treats to nearby Dolores Park. Expect to spend around $10 to $20 per person.

Sam's Chowder House

Sam's Chowder House, with a location in Half Moon Bay, is famous for its seafood dishes, especially the New England-style clam chowder and lobster rolls. The Pier 39 location is easily accessible by the F-Market & Wharves streetcar and various MUNI bus lines. It is open daily from 11:00 AM to 9:00 PM.

Website

Sam's Chowder House

The restaurant offers a casual dining experience with stunning views of the bay. The menu features a variety of seafood dishes, from chowder to grilled fish, catering to both seafood lovers and those seeking more traditional American fare. Prices range from $20 to $40 per meal.

Bi-Rite Creamery

For a sweet treat, Bi-Rite Creamery at 3692 18th Street in the Mission District offers some of the best ice cream in the city. Known for its organic, locally sourced ingredients, this creamery creates unique flavors like salted caramel and honey lavender. To get there, you can take the 14-Mission or 33-Stanyan MUNI bus lines. The creamery is open daily from 11:00 AM to 10:00 PM.

The casual, family-friendly atmosphere makes it a popular spot for both locals and tourists. The creamy, rich ice cream is reasonably priced, with most servings costing around $5 to $10. There's often a line, but the wait is worth it for a taste of their delicious ice cream.

San Francisco's casual dining spots offer a wide range of delicious options, from classic Mexican fare and artisan pizza to fresh seafood and mouth-watering desserts. These restaurants provide a taste of the city's vibrant food scene.

Budget-Friendly Dining

San Francisco, known for its diverse culinary scene, offers plenty of budget-friendly dining options that allow both locals and tourists to enjoy delicious meals without breaking the bank. Here are some of the best spots where you can savor quality food at affordable prices.

Taqueria El Farolito

Taqueria El Farolito, located at 2779 Mission Street in the Mission District, is a beloved spot for authentic Mexican food. Known for its generous portions and flavorful dishes, this taqueria is a favorite among locals and visitors. To get there, you can take the 14-Mission or 49-Van Ness-Mission MUNI bus lines. The restaurant is open daily from 10:00 AM to 2:30 AM, making it a great option for late-night dining.

Website

El Farolito Mexican Restaurant San Francisco

The menu features a variety of Mexican staples, including burritos, tacos, quesadillas, and tortas. The super burrito, stuffed with your choice of meat, rice, beans, and fresh toppings, is particularly popular. Expect to spend around $10 to $15 per meal. The casual and lively atmosphere caters to a diverse crowd, from families to night owls looking for a satisfying meal.

Golden Boy Pizza

Golden Boy Pizza, located at 542 Green Street in North Beach, is famous for its Sicilian-style pizza. This small, family-owned pizzeria has been serving up delicious slices since 1978. To get there, you can take the 8-Bayshore or 30-Stockton MUNI bus lines. Golden Boy Pizza is open Tuesday to Thursday from 11:30 AM to 10:00 PM, Friday and Saturday from 11:30 AM to 1:00 AM, and Sunday from 11:30 AM to 9:00 PM.

Website

Golden Boy Pizza

The menu includes a variety of pizza slices, with the clam and garlic pizza being a standout favorite. The casual setting and quick service make it an ideal spot for a quick bite or a relaxed meal with friends. Prices range from $4 to $5 per slice, making it an affordable choice for pizza lovers.

Sam Wo Restaurant

Sam Wo Restaurant, located at 713 Clay Street in Chinatown, is a historic eatery that has been serving traditional Chinese food since 1907. Known for its late-night hours and delicious dishes, Sam Wo is a popular spot for budget-friendly dining. To get there, you can take the 1-California or 8-Bayshore MUNI bus lines. The restaurant is open Monday to Thursday from 11:00 AM to 10:00 PM, Friday and Saturday from 11:00 AM to 3:00 AM, and Sunday from 11:00 AM to 10:00 PM.

Website

Sam Wo Restaurant

The menu features a variety of Chinese dishes, including barbecue pork rice noodle rolls, wonton soup, and chow mein. Prices are very reasonable, with most meals costing around $10 to $15. The casual atmosphere and friendly service make it a great spot for both locals and tourists.

Red's Java House

Red's Java House, located at Pier 30, is a classic waterfront diner known for its simple, hearty meals and stunning views of the Bay Bridge. This no-frills eatery has been a staple in San Francisco since the 1950s. To get there, you can take the N-Judah MUNI light rail or the F-Market & Wharves streetcar. Red's Java House is open daily from 7:00 AM to 5:00 PM.

Website

Red's Java House

The menu includes classic American fare such as burgers, hot dogs, and fish and chips. The cheeseburger, served on a sourdough roll, is a must-try. Prices range from $5 to $15 per meal. The laid-back vibe and scenic location make it a popular spot for a casual meal by the bay.

Saigon Sandwich

Saigon Sandwich, located at 560 Larkin Street in the Tenderloin, is famous for its delicious and affordable banh mi sandwiches. This small Vietnamese deli is a local favorite for quick, budget-friendly meals. To get there, you can take the 19-Polk or 31-Balboa MUNI bus lines. Saigon Sandwich is open Monday to Saturday from 7:00 AM to 5:00 PM.

The menu features a variety of banh mi options, including roast pork, chicken, and tofu, all served on freshly baked baguettes with pickled vegetables and cilantro. Prices are incredibly affordable, with most sandwiches costing around $5. The no-frills atmosphere and speedy service make it a great spot for a quick, tasty meal.

Arizmendi Bakery

Arizmendi Bakery, located at 1331 9th Avenue in the Inner Sunset, is a worker-owned cooperative known for its fresh-baked goods and delicious pizza. To get there, you can take the N-Judah MUNI light rail. The bakery is open daily from 7:00 AM to 7:00 PM.

Website

Arizmendi Bakery

The menu includes a variety of baked goods, from scones and muffins to breads and cookies. The daily pizza, made with fresh, organic ingredients, is a highlight. Prices are reasonable, with most items costing under $10. The cozy, welcoming atmosphere makes it a perfect spot for a casual breakfast or lunch.

San Francisco offers a wealth of budget-friendly dining options that allow you to enjoy the city's diverse culinary scene without spending a fortune.

Street Food

San Francisco is a haven for street food enthusiasts, offering an eclectic mix of flavors and cuisines that reflect the city's diverse cultural tapestry. From food trucks to market stalls, here are some of the best street food spots that both locals and tourists love.

Off the Grid

Off the Grid is a roaming mobile food extravaganza that brings together some of the best food trucks and vendors in the Bay Area. The flagship event takes place at Fort Mason Center, 2 Marina Boulevard, San Francisco, CA

94123. To get there, you can take the 30-Stockton or 22-Fillmore MUNI bus lines. Off the Grid at Fort Mason operates every Friday evening from 5:00 PM to 10:00 PM, offering a vibrant atmosphere with live music, communal seating, and a variety of food options.

The event features a rotating lineup of food trucks and vendors, offering everything from Korean BBQ tacos to gourmet grilled cheese sandwiches and artisanal desserts. The casual, festive atmosphere attracts a diverse crowd, including families, young professionals, and tourists. Prices vary by vendor but generally range from $10 to $20 per meal. Expect long lines for popular trucks, but the wait is often worth it for the delicious food and lively ambiance.

SOMA StrEat Food Park

SOMA StrEat Food Park, located at 428 11th Street, is a permanent food truck park that hosts a variety of vendors in a fun, laid-back environment. To get there, you can take the 9-San Bruno or 47-Van Ness MUNI bus lines. The park is open daily from 11:00 AM to 3:00 PM and from 5:00 PM to 9:00 PM.

The park features a rotating selection of food trucks, offering diverse cuisines such as Mexican, Filipino, Japanese, and American comfort food. In addition to the food trucks, the park has seating areas, restrooms, and often hosts special events like trivia nights and live music. The casual setting and affordable prices, typically $10 to $15 per meal, make it a popular spot for both locals and tourists looking for a quick, tasty bite.

The Chairman Truck

The Chairman Truck is one of San Francisco's most popular food trucks, known for its flavorful steamed and baked buns filled with a variety of savory ingredients. The truck roams the city but has regular stops.

The menu features items like pork belly buns with pickled daikon, spicy chicken buns, and tofu buns with miso greens. The Chairman Truck caters to a wide audience, from office workers on lunch breaks to tourists exploring the city. Prices are reasonable, with most items costing around $5 to $10. The truck's vibrant red design makes it easy to spot, and the food's bold flavors keep customers coming back.

Ferry Building Marketplace

The Ferry Building Marketplace, located at One Ferry Building, is not just a hub for commuters but also a destination for food lovers. To get there, you can take the BART to the Embarcadero Station or the F-Market & Wharves streetcar. The marketplace is open daily, with most vendors operating from 10:00 AM to 6:00 PM.

Inside the historic Ferry Building, you'll find a variety of food stalls and kiosks offering street food-style eats. Highlights include the empanadas at El Porteno, the artisan bread at Acme Bread Company, and the oysters at Hog Island Oyster Company. The marketplace caters to a diverse crowd, including locals, tourists, and office workers. Prices vary but generally range from $10 to $20 per meal. The lively environment and waterfront views make it a delightful place to enjoy a meal.

Roli Roti

Roli Roti, known as the first gourmet rotisserie food truck, offers succulent rotisserie chicken and pork served with fresh sides. The truck's regular location is at the Ferry Plaza Farmers Market, One Ferry Building, on Tuesdays, Thursdays, and Saturdays. To get there, you can take the BART to the Embarcadero Station or the F-Market & Wharves streetcar.

The menu features items like rotisserie chicken with rosemary potatoes, porchetta sandwiches, and seasonal salads. Roli Roti caters to a wide range of people, from foodies and families to office workers and tourists. Prices are reasonable, with most meals costing around $10 to $15. The high-quality ingredients and delicious flavors make Roli Roti a must-try.

San Francisco's street food scene offers a wide array of culinary delights, from gourmet food trucks to bustling marketplaces. These street food spots provide delicious, affordable options that showcase the city's diverse flavors and vibrant food culture.

Cafes and Bakeries

San Francisco is renowned for its eclectic mix of cafes and bakeries, offering everything from artisanal coffee to mouth-watering pastries. These establishments are not just places to grab a quick bite; they are integral parts of the city's vibrant culture, providing cozy spots for locals and tourists to relax, work, and socialize. Here's a look at some of the best cafes and bakeries in San Francisco, beloved by both residents and visitors.

Tartine Bakery

Tartine Bakery, located at 600 Guerrero Street in the Mission District, is a must-visit for anyone with a love for high-quality baked goods. Known for its artisanal bread and pastries, Tartine has earned a reputation for its commitment to using the finest ingredients. To get there, you can take the J-Church MUNI light rail or the 14-Mission bus line. The bakery is open daily from 7:30 AM to 8:00 PM.

At Tartine, you can expect to find a variety of fresh pastries, including their famous morning buns, croissants, and pain au chocolat. They also offer a selection of sandwiches and coffee. The cozy, bustling atmosphere attracts a diverse crowd, from food enthusiasts to tourists exploring the Mission District. Prices range from $3 to $15, making it a reasonably affordable option for a quality meal or snack.

Blue Bottle Coffee

Blue Bottle Coffee, with multiple locations across San Francisco, is a favorite among coffee aficionados. The Ferry Building location at One Ferry Building is particularly popular. Accessible via the BART to the Embarcadero Station or the F-Market & Wharves streetcar, Blue Bottle is open Monday to Friday from 6:30 AM to 7:00 PM and weekends from 8:00 AM to 6:00 PM.

Blue Bottle is known for its meticulously crafted coffee, sourced from sustainable farms and roasted to perfection. The minimalist, modern décor provides a relaxing environment for enjoying a cup of pour-over coffee, espresso, or a selection of pastries. The café caters to a wide range of customers, from busy professionals to tourists seeking a high-quality caffeine fix. Expect to spend around $4 to $10 per item.

Boudin Bakery

Boudin Bakery, located at 160 Jefferson Street in Fisherman's Wharf, is a historic San Francisco institution famous for its sourdough bread. To get there, you can take the Powell-Hyde cable car or the 19-Polk MUNI bus line. The bakery is open daily from 8:00 AM to 9:00 PM.

At Boudin, you can enjoy a variety of sourdough-based dishes, including clam chowder in a bread bowl, sandwiches, and pizzas. The bakery also offers a café with coffee and pastries. The lively atmosphere and waterfront views make it a great spot for families and tourists. Prices range from $5 to $20, depending on the meal.

Arizmendi Bakery

Arizmendi Bakery, located at 1331 9th Avenue in the Inner Sunset, is a worker-owned cooperative known for its fresh-baked goods and delicious pizza. To get there, you can take the N-Judah MUNI light rail. The bakery is open daily from 7:00 AM to 7:00 PM.

The menu includes a variety of baked goods, such as scones, muffins, cookies, and their daily pizza, made with fresh, organic ingredients. The community-focused atmosphere and affordable prices, typically under $10, attract a mix of locals, students, and visitors exploring Golden Gate Park nearby.

Ritual Coffee Roasters

Ritual Coffee Roasters, located at 1026 Valencia Street, is a staple in San Francisco's coffee scene. Known for its dedication to quality and sustainability, Ritual sources its beans directly from farmers around the world. To get there, you can take the 14-Mission or 49-Van Ness-Mission MUNI bus lines. The café is open daily from 7:00 AM to 6:00 PM.

Ritual offers a variety of coffee drinks, including pour-overs, espresso, and cold brew, along with a selection of pastries. The modern, airy space is perfect for both working and socializing, attracting a hip, young crowd. Prices range from $3 to $8, making it an affordable spot for a quality coffee experience.

Sightglass Coffee

Sightglass Coffee, with its flagship location at 270 7th Street in SoMa, is a third-wave coffee roaster known for its high-quality beans and inviting atmosphere. To get there, you can take the 9-San Bruno or 19-Polk MUNI bus lines. The café is open Monday to Friday from 7:00 AM to 6:00 PM and weekends from 8:00 AM to 6:00 PM.

Sightglass offers a range of coffee drinks, from meticulously brewed pour-overs to rich espressos. The spacious, industrial-style café provides a great environment for both working and socializing. Prices are in the range of $4 to $10, making it a popular spot for coffee enthusiasts.

Tips for Visiting San Francisco's Cafes and Bakeries

Arrive Early

Popular spots like Tartine Bakery can get crowded, so arriving early can help you avoid long lines.

Explore Different Neighborhoods

Each area of San Francisco has its unique charm and specialty cafes, so take the opportunity to explore different parts of the city.

Take Your Time

Many cafes offer a relaxed atmosphere perfect for unwinding, working, or catching up with friends, so don't rush through your visit.

Try the Local Specialties

Each bakery and café often has signature items or seasonal specials, so be sure to ask the staff for recommendations.

San Francisco's cafes and bakeries offer a delightful mix of artisanal coffee, fresh pastries, and inviting atmospheres. Whether you're looking for a quick caffeine fix, a leisurely breakfast, or a place to unwind, these spots provide a taste of the city's vibrant culinary culture.

Bars And Pubs

San Francisco's vibrant nightlife scene is home to an eclectic mix of bars and pubs, each offering its own unique ambiance and specialties. Whether you're looking for a chic cocktail lounge, a cozy pub with craft beers, or a lively sports bar, the city has something to suit every taste. Here's a guide to some of the best bars and pubs in San Francisco that both locals and tourists enjoy.

Toronado

Toronado, located at 547 Haight Street in the Lower Haight, is a legendary beer bar known for its extensive selection of craft brews. Established in 1987, Toronado has become a staple for beer enthusiasts. To get there, you can take the N-Judah MUNI light rail or the 6-Haight/Parnassus bus line. The bar is open daily from 11:30 AM to 2:00 AM.

Toronado offers a rotating list of over 40 beers on tap, including local favorites and rare international finds. The bar caters to a diverse crowd, from craft beer aficionados to casual drinkers. The no-frills, laid-back atmosphere makes it a perfect spot for enjoying a pint with friends. Prices are reasonable, with most beers costing between $6 and $10. Note that Toronado is a cash-only establishment, so be prepared.

Trick Dog

Trick Dog, located at 3010 20th Street in the Mission District, is renowned for its creative cocktails and trendy ambiance. This bar consistently ranks among the best cocktail bars in the country. To get there, you can take the 14-Mission or 49-Van Ness/Mission MUNI bus lines. Trick Dog is open Monday to Friday from 3:00 PM to 2:00 AM and weekends from 2:00 PM to 2:00 AM.

The menu, which changes regularly, features inventive cocktails with quirky names and high-quality ingredients. Trick Dog also offers a selection of bar snacks and small plates. The stylish, artistic décor and friendly bartenders create a lively and welcoming atmosphere. Prices for cocktails range from $12 to $16. Expect a mix of locals and tourists, especially on weekends when it can get quite busy.

The Buena Vista Cafe

The Buena Vista Cafe, located at 2765 Hyde Street, is famous for introducing Irish coffee to the United States. This historic bar has been a fixture since 1916 and continues to draw crowds for its signature drink. To get there, you can take the Powell-Hyde cable car or the 19-Polk MUNI bus line. The Buena Vista is open daily from 8:00 AM to 2:00 AM.

The menu includes a variety of cocktails, wines, and beers, but the star of the show is the Irish coffee, made with hot coffee, Irish whiskey, sugar, and a float of cream. The café also serves a full menu of American comfort food, making it a great spot for brunch or a late-night meal. Prices are moderate, with most drinks costing around $10 to $12. The warm, inviting atmosphere caters to all kinds of patrons, from tourists to locals enjoying a classic drink.

Monk's Kettle

Monk's Kettle, located at 3141 16th Street in the Mission District, is a cozy gastropub known for its impressive beer list and upscale pub fare. To get there, you can take the 22-Fillmore or 33-Stanyan MUNI bus lines. The bar is open Monday to Thursday from 12:00 PM to 12:00 AM, Friday from 12:00 PM to 1:00 AM, Saturday from 11:00 AM to 1:00 AM, and Sunday from 11:00 AM to 12:00 AM.

Monk's Kettle offers over 200 bottled beers and 28 rotating taps, focusing on craft and rare brews. The menu features elevated pub food, including items like duck confit poutine, burgers, and seasonal salads. The intimate, rustic atmosphere and knowledgeable staff make it a favorite for beer lovers and foodies alike. Prices range from $8 to $15 for beers and $15 to $25 for food.

Smuggler's Cove

Smuggler's Cove, located at 650 Gough Street in the Hayes Valley, is a tiki bar that transports patrons to a tropical paradise. Known for its extensive rum selection and elaborate tiki cocktails, Smuggler's Cove offers a unique drinking experience. To get there, you can take the 21-Hayes or 5-Fulton MUNI bus lines. The bar is open Monday to Saturday from 5:00 PM to 12:00 AM and Sunday from 5:00 PM to 11:00 PM.

The menu features a variety of classic and original tiki drinks, all made with high-quality ingredients and served in decorative mugs. The immersive décor, complete with tiki statues and nautical artifacts, creates a fun and festive atmosphere. Cocktails are priced between $12 and $15. Smuggler's Cove attracts a lively crowd, making it a great spot for a fun night out.

Tips for Enjoying San Francisco's Bars and Pubs

Plan Ahead

Popular spots like Trick Dog and Smuggler's Cove can get crowded, so it's wise to arrive early or plan for a wait.

Know the Rules

Some bars, like Toronado, are cash-only. Always check ahead and be prepared.

Dress Code

While most bars in San Francisco are casual, some upscale spots may have a dress code. Check the bar's website or call ahead if you're unsure.

Enjoy Responsibly

San Francisco has excellent public transportation and ride-sharing options, so there's no need to drive if you're planning to drink.

San Francisco's bars and pubs offer a rich and diverse nightlife experience, these spots provide a welcoming atmosphere and high-quality drinks that reflect the city's vibrant culture.

Nightclubs and Live Music Venues

San Francisco's nightlife scene is vibrant and diverse, offering a range of nightclubs and live music venues that cater to different tastes and preferences. Whether you're into electronic dance music, live jazz, or indie rock, the city has something to keep you entertained well into the night. Here are some of the best nightclubs and live music venues in San Francisco.

1015 Folsom

1015 Folsom is one of San Francisco's premier nightclubs, known for its large dance floors, top-notch sound system, and an eclectic lineup of DJs and live acts. Located at 1015 Folsom Street in SoMa, the club is easily accessible via the BART to Civic Center Station or the 14-Mission MUNI bus line. 1015 Folsom is open Friday and Saturday from 10:00 PM to 3:00 AM.

The venue features multiple rooms, each with its own unique vibe and music style, ranging from EDM and hip-hop to techno and house. The club attracts a diverse crowd, including locals and visitors looking for a high-energy night out. Tickets typically range from $20 to $40, depending on the event. Expect a lively atmosphere with state-of-the-art lighting and sound systems that create an immersive experience.

The Independent

The Independent is a popular live music venue located at 628 Divisadero Street in the Western Addition. Known for its intimate setting and excellent acoustics, The Independent hosts a variety of artists, from emerging indie bands to established acts across genres. To get there, you can take the 5-Fulton or 24-Divisadero MUNI bus lines. The venue is open most nights, with doors typically opening at 8:00 PM.

The Independent has a standing-room-only policy, which adds to the intimate concert experience. The bar offers a selection of beers, wines, and cocktails, and while there is no kitchen, food trucks often park outside to serve concert-goers. Ticket prices generally range from $20 to $50, depending on the artist. The venue caters to a wide range of music lovers, making it a favorite spot for catching live performances in an up-close setting.

Bimbo's 365 Club

Bimbo's 365 Club, located at 1025 Columbus Avenue in North Beach, is a historic venue that has been a staple of San Francisco's nightlife since 1931. Known for its Art Deco decor and vintage charm, Bimbo's hosts a variety of events, including live music, burlesque shows, and private parties. To get there, you can take the 30-Stockton or 45-Union/Stockton MUNI bus lines. The club is open on event nights, usually starting around 8:00 PM.

The venue features a full bar and offers a range of cocktails, wines, and beers. The elegant setting attracts a mix of locals and tourists looking for a unique and nostalgic nightlife experience. Ticket prices vary widely depending on the event, but they generally range from $30 to $60. Expect a classy, sophisticated atmosphere with top-notch performances and a touch of old-school glamour.

DNA Lounge

DNA Lounge is a versatile venue located at 375 11th Street in SoMa, known for its diverse programming that includes dance nights, live music, and even all-ages events. The venue features two stages, a pizzeria, and a full bar, making it a popular spot for a night out. To get there, you can take the 9-San Bruno or 12-Folsom/Pacific MUNI bus lines. DNA Lounge is open most nights, with events starting around 9:00 PM.

The venue caters to a wide range of tastes, with events ranging from goth and industrial nights to hip-hop and electronic music. The bar offers a selection of drinks, and the on-site pizza kitchen is open late. Tickets typically range from $10 to $30, making it an affordable option for a fun night out. The casual, inclusive atmosphere attracts a diverse crowd, including music enthusiasts and club-goers.

The Fillmore

The Fillmore, located at 1805 Geary Boulevard in the Western Addition, is one of San Francisco's most iconic live music venues. Known for its rich history and legendary performances, The Fillmore continues to host a wide range of artists across genres. To get there, you can take the 22-Fillmore or 38-Geary MUNI bus lines. The venue is open on event nights, with doors typically opening at 7:00 PM.

The Fillmore offers a full bar and a selection of snacks, and it's famous for giving out free apples to concert-goers. The venue is primarily standing-room, though there are a few seats available on a first-come, first-served basis. Ticket prices generally range from $30 to $70, depending on the artist. The Fillmore attracts a diverse audience, from die-hard music fans to those looking to experience a piece of San Francisco's musical history. The intimate setting and excellent acoustics make it a fantastic place to catch a live show.

Tips for Enjoying San Francisco's Nightclubs and Music Venues

Plan Ahead

Popular venues like The Fillmore and The Independent often sell out, so it's best to buy tickets in advance.

Arrive Early

For general admission shows, arriving early can help you secure a good spot close to the stage.

Dress Code

While most venues have a casual dress code, some nightclubs might have specific requirements. Check the venue's website for details.

Stay Safe

Use public transportation or ride-sharing services if you plan to drink. San Francisco has excellent options, making it easy to get around safely.

San Francisco's nightclubs and live music venues offer a vibrant and eclectic nightlife experience.

Wine Bars and Breweries

San Francisco's wine bars and breweries offer a delightful exploration of local and international flavors, making them perfect spots for unwinding and socializing. Whether you're a wine connoisseur or a craft beer enthusiast, the city provides a plethora of options that cater to a diverse clientele. Here's a guide to some of the best wine bars and breweries in San Francisco.

Wine Bars

The Barrel Room

The Barrel Room, located at 415 Sansome Street, is a cozy wine bar known for its extensive selection of wines from around the world. The ambiance is warm and inviting, making it a perfect spot for both casual and romantic evenings. To get there, you can take the BART to Embarcadero Station or the MUNI 1-California bus line. The Barrel Room is open Monday to Friday from 4:00 PM to 10:00 PM.

The wine list at The Barrel Room changes regularly, focusing on different regions and themes each month. The menu includes a variety of small plates and charcuterie that pair perfectly with the wines. Prices for wines by the glass range from $10 to $20, while bottles can go from $30 to over $100. The venue attracts a mix of locals and tourists, from wine aficionados to those simply looking to enjoy a good glass of wine in a relaxed setting.

Press Club

Press Club, situated at 20 Yerba Buena Lane, is an upscale wine bar offering a sophisticated experience. Located in the heart of downtown, it's easily accessible via the Powell Street BART Station or several MUNI lines. The Press Club is open Tuesday to Saturday from 4:00 PM to 10:00 PM.

This elegant venue features an extensive selection of wines and craft beers, along with artisanal cheeses and charcuterie. The chic, modern décor makes it a popular spot for both business gatherings and date nights. Wine flights are available for those looking to sample a variety of wines, with prices ranging from $15 to $40. The clientele includes professionals, tourists, and local wine lovers, all enjoying the refined atmosphere and top-notch service.

Breweries

Anchor Brewing Company

Anchor Brewing Company, located in Potrero Hill, is one of the oldest craft breweries in the United States. Established in 1896, it has become a cornerstone of San Francisco's brewing history. To get there, you can take the 19-Polk or 22-Fillmore MUNI bus lines. The brewery is open for tours and tastings Tuesday to Saturday from 11:00 AM to 6:00 PM.

The brewery offers guided tours that provide insight into the brewing process and the history of Anchor Brewing.

Visitors can sample a variety of beers, including their famous Anchor Steam Beer, Liberty Ale, and seasonal brews. The tasting room offers a casual and friendly environment, attracting both beer enthusiasts and tourists. Tours cost around $25 per person, including tastings.

Tips for Enjoying Wine Bars and Breweries

Check Schedules

Some wine bars and breweries offer special events, tastings, or happy hours, so check their websites for the latest updates.

Reserve Tours

For brewery tours, it's often a good idea to book in advance, especially for popular spots like Anchor Brewing Company.

Try Flights

Many places offer wine or beer flights, which are a great way to sample a variety of options without committing to a full glass.

Plan Your Transport

San Francisco has excellent public transportation and ride-sharing options, making it easy to enjoy your drinks responsibly.

The wine bars and breweries offer a vibrant and diverse nightlife experience, providing opportunities to explore a wide range of flavors in welcoming and unique settings.

San Francisco's culinary scene and nightlife offer endless opportunities for exploration and enjoyment. The city pulses with energy, providing unique experiences at every turn.

CHAPTER 11

Shopping

San Francisco is a shopper's paradise, offering a diverse array of retail experiences that cater to every taste and budget. The city's shopping scene is as varied and dynamic as its cultural landscape. Here's a guide to some of the best shopping destinations in San Francisco.

Union Square

Union Square is the heart of San Francisco's shopping district, home to an array of high-end department stores, luxury boutiques, and flagship stores. Located at the intersection of Geary, Powell, Post, and Stockton Streets, Union Square is easily accessible by the Powell Street BART Station and various MUNI lines. Most stores in the area are open daily from 10:00 AM to 8:00 PM.

In Union Square, you can find iconic department stores like Macy's, Neiman Marcus, and Saks Fifth Avenue, alongside luxury brands such as Louis Vuitton, Gucci, and Chanel. Also, check out Maiden Lane. The square itself is often bustling with street performers, art installations, and seasonal decorations, creating a lively atmosphere. Shoppers can expect to spend from moderate to high amounts, depending on the stores they visit. Union Square also offers a variety of dining options, from casual cafes to fine dining restaurants, making it a perfect spot to spend a full day.

Ferry Building Marketplace

The Ferry Building Marketplace, located at One Ferry Building on the Embarcadero, is a must-visit for foodies and those looking for unique, locally-made products. To get there, you can take the BART to the Embarcadero Station or the F-Market & Wharves streetcar. The marketplace is open Monday to Friday from 10:00 AM to 6:00 PM, Saturday from 8:00 AM to 6:00 PM, and Sunday from 11:00 AM to 5:00 PM.

Inside the historic Ferry Building, you'll find an array of artisanal food vendors, specialty shops, and restaurants. Highlights include the Cowgirl Creamery for artisanal cheeses, Acme Bread Company for fresh-baked bread, and Heath Ceramics for beautifully crafted pottery. The bustling farmers' market on Tuesdays, Thursdays, and Saturdays adds to the vibrant atmosphere. Prices vary, but expect to find premium products worth every penny. The Ferry Building also offers stunning waterfront views, making it a pleasant place to shop and dine.

Haight-Ashbury

Haight-Ashbury, famous for its role in the 1960s counterculture movement, is a vibrant neighborhood filled with eclectic shops and vintage stores. The main shopping area is along Haight Street, between Stanyan Street and Masonic Avenue. To get there, you can take the 7-Haight/Noriega or 43-Masonic MUNI bus lines. Most stores are open daily from 11:00 AM to 7:00 PM.

In Haight-Ashbury, you can expect to find a mix of vintage clothing stores, record shops, and quirky boutiques. Notable spots include Amoeba Music, one of the largest independent music stores in the world, and Decades of Fashion, offering vintage clothing from the 1880s to the 1980s. The area attracts a diverse crowd, from tourists and hippie enthusiasts to local fashionistas. Prices range from affordable to moderate, depending on the store and item. The vibrant street art and historic architecture add to the neighborhood's unique charm.

Chinatown

San Francisco's Chinatown is the oldest and one of the largest in North America, offering a rich array of shops, markets, and restaurants. The main shopping area is along Grant Avenue and Stockton Street, between Bush Street and Broadway. To get there, you can take the 1-California or 30-Stockton MUNI bus lines. Most stores are open daily from 10:00 AM to 8:00 PM.

Chinatown is a great place to find unique gifts, traditional Chinese medicine, herbs, and spices, as well as beautiful jade jewelry and ornate home décor. Popular spots include the Golden Gate Fortune Cookie Factory, where you can watch fortune cookies being made, and China Live, a modern marketplace offering gourmet food and high-quality kitchenware. Prices in Chinatown are generally affordable, and the bustling streets and colorful lanterns make for an exciting shopping experience.

Fillmore Street

Fillmore Street, running through the Pacific Heights neighborhood, is a charming shopping destination known for its mix of high-end boutiques, trendy shops, and cozy cafes. The main shopping area is between Jackson Street and Eddy Street. To get there, you can take the 22-Fillmore MUNI bus line. Most stores are open daily from 10:00 AM to 7:00 PM.

Fillmore Street offers a more relaxed shopping experience with stores like Alice + Olivia, Jonathan Adler, and Rebecca Minkoff, alongside unique local boutiques. The area also boasts a variety of dining options, from gourmet restaurants to casual eateries. Prices range from moderate to high, reflecting the upscale nature of the neighborhood. The tree-lined streets and historic Victorian architecture add to the appeal, making it a pleasant area to explore on foot.

Hayes Valley

Hayes Valley is a trendy neighborhood known for its independent boutiques, artisanal shops, and vibrant food scene. The main shopping area is along Hayes Street, between Laguna and Franklin Streets. To get there, you can take the 21-Hayes or 5-Fulton MUNI bus lines. Most stores are open daily from 11:00 AM to 7:00 PM.

In Hayes Valley, you can expect to find a curated selection of fashion, home décor, and art. Notable stores include Azalea, a boutique offering stylish clothing and accessories, and Maker & Moss, featuring handcrafted furniture and home goods. The area attracts a hip, youthful crowd, and prices range from moderate to high. Hayes Valley also offers a variety of trendy cafes and wine bars, making it a great spot for a leisurely day of shopping and dining.

Tips for Shopping In San Francisco

Public Transportation

San Francisco has excellent public transportation, so consider using BART, MUNI, or cable cars to get around.

Dress in Layers

The weather can change quickly, so dressing in layers will keep you comfortable as you shop.

Carry Cash

Some smaller shops and vendors, especially in markets, may prefer cash.

Explore Different Neighborhoods

Each area has its own unique vibe and offerings, so take the time to explore multiple shopping districts.

San Francisco's shopping scene offers something for everyone, whether you're looking for luxury brands, unique local finds, or budget-friendly options. With its diverse array of neighborhoods and shopping experiences, the city provides endless opportunities for retail therapy.

CHAPTER 12

Cultural Experiences

San Francisco is a city rich in culture and history, offering a wide range of experiences that reflect its diverse population and artistic spirit. The city's cultural landscape is shaped by its numerous festivals, vibrant arts scene, historical landmarks, and eclectic neighborhoods. You'll find plenty of opportunities to immerse yourself in the unique character and traditions that define San Francisco. This chapter will introduce you to some of the most enriching cultural experiences the city has to offer, ensuring a memorable and insightful visit.

Festivals and Events

San Francisco's cultural calendar is rich with festivals and events that showcase the city's diverse heritage and vibrant community spirit. These celebrations span a variety of interests, from music and food to parades and cultural exhibitions, making them an integral part of the city's cultural experience.

Chinese New Year Parade

The Chinese New Year Parade is a spectacular celebration that takes place in late January or early February, marking the Lunar New Year. The event kicks off in the evening and features elaborate floats, lion dancers, and the famous Golden Dragon. Spectators should dress warmly and wear comfortable shoes, as they will be standing for an extended period. It's a good idea to bring a camera to capture the vibrant festivities and some cash for the street vendors selling traditional snacks and souvenirs.

Outside Lands Music and Arts Festival

Held annually in August in Golden Gate Park, the Outside Lands Music and Arts Festival is a major draw for music lovers and foodies alike. The festival runs for three days and features a diverse lineup of musical acts, along with art installations and gourmet food and drink options. Comfortable, layered clothing and sturdy shoes are recommended due to the park's variable weather. Essentials to bring include a refillable water bottle, sunscreen, and a portable phone charger.

San Francisco Pride

San Francisco Pride is one of the largest LGBTQ+ celebrations in the world, taking place on the last weekend of June. The event includes a colorful parade down Market Street and a two-day festival in Civic Center Plaza. Attendees typically wear vibrant, expressive clothing with rainbow-themed accessories. Comfortable footwear is essential for the parade, and it's wise to bring water, sunscreen, and some cash for vendors.

Hardly Strictly Bluegrass

Hardly Strictly Bluegrass is a free music festival held every October in Golden Gate Park. This event features a mix of bluegrass, folk, and Americana music, attracting a large and diverse audience. Performances usually run from noon to 7:00 PM each day. Casual, layered clothing is recommended due to the park's changing weather, and attendees should bring a blanket or low-back chair, a refillable water bottle, and snacks.

Fleet Week

San Francisco Fleet Week occurs in October, honoring the U.S. armed forces with a series of events, including air shows by the Blue Angels, ship tours, and military demonstrations. The air shows typically happen from 12:00 PM to 4:00 PM over the weekend. Attendees should dress casually and in layers, and bring binoculars, a camera, sunscreen, a hat, and a jacket. Snacks and water are also advisable due to the large crowds at food vendors.

Cherry Blossom Festival

The Northern California Cherry Blossom Festival, held over two weekends in April in Japantown, celebrates Japanese culture with traditional music, dance, and cuisine. Visitors can expect to see Taiko drummers, martial arts demonstrations, and enjoy a variety of Japanese foods. Comfortable, casual clothing is recommended, though traditional attire like a kimono is also appropriate. Essentials to bring include a camera, cash for vendors, a water bottle, and sunscreen.

Bay to Breakers

Bay to Breakers is a historic footrace held in May, where participants run from the Bay to the Pacific Ocean, often in elaborate costumes. The race is not only a competitive event but also an all-day party. Runners and spectators alike should dress in comfortable, weather-appropriate clothing. Bringing water, snacks, and a camera is recommended to capture the unique and festive atmosphere.

San Francisco's festivals and events provide a vivid and engaging way to experience the city's diverse culture and community spirit. These celebrations are not only about entertainment but also about bringing people together to enjoy the unique aspects of San Francisco's vibrant life.

Performing Arts

San Francisco's performing arts scene is a vibrant and integral part of the city's cultural fabric, offering a rich tapestry of theater, music, and dance performances. Here's a look at each category, highlighting some of the key venues.

Theater

San Francisco boasts a dynamic theater scene, with a range of performances from Broadway hits to avant-garde productions. The American Conservatory Theater (ACT) is a cornerstone, presenting high-quality productions at the Toni Rembe Theatre and the Strand Theatre near Union Square. Notable upcoming performances include "Big Data" and "A Strange Loop" in 2024. These venues are easily accessible via public transportation, including BART and MUNI, making them convenient for both locals and tourists.

Another key player is the San Francisco Playhouse, located on Post Street. This mid-size theater offers an Off-Broadway lineup in an intimate setting, with upcoming shows like "The 39 Steps" and "Evita" scheduled for 2024. The New Conservatory Theatre Center on Van Ness Avenue focuses on creating high-quality productions and educational experiences, particularly for queer and allied communities, with shows like "Unpacking in P'Town" and "Tick, Tick… BOOM!".

Music

San Francisco's music scene is equally impressive, featuring a broad spectrum of performances ranging from classical to contemporary genres. The San Francisco Symphony, performing at Davies Symphony Hall, is renowned for its world-class concerts. Located in the Civic Center neighborhood, the hall is easily accessible by BART and various MUNI lines. The 2024 season includes a diverse lineup of performances under the baton of Edwin Outwater, with programs featuring works by Grieg, Bruckner, and contemporary composers like Ellen Reid.

San Francisco Performances, another significant entity, offers a series of concerts at venues such as the Herbst Theatre and the SFJAZZ Center. Their 2024-25 season features a mix of chamber music, piano recitals, and innovative new works, catering to a wide range of musical tastes. The San Francisco Conservatory of Music (SFCM) also plays a vital role, presenting over 500 performances annually, including student recitals, faculty concerts, and guest artist series at the Ann Getty Center for Education.

Dance

San Francisco's dance scene is highlighted by prestigious companies like the San Francisco Ballet, one of the oldest professional ballet companies in the United States. Performances are held at the War Memorial Opera House, located in the Civic Center area. The ballet's 2024 season includes classics like "Giselle" and contemporary works, offering something for every dance enthusiast.

Additionally, venues like the Presidio Theatre and the Yerba Buena Center for the Arts host a variety of dance performances throughout the year, including modern dance, flamenco, and international dance festivals. These performances showcase the city's commitment to diverse and innovative dance expressions, providing audiences with a rich array of styles and experiences.

San Francisco's performing arts venues are spread throughout the city, making them accessible and convenient for visitors. When attending these events, it's advisable to dress smart-casual unless otherwise specified, and to check the specific venue's guidelines for any additional rules. Bringing a sweater or light jacket is recommended due to the city's cool evenings. Tickets can be purchased online through the respective venues' websites, with many offering subscription packages for regular attendees.

Exploring San Francisco's theater, music, and dance scenes provides an immersive cultural experience, highlighting the city's artistic excellence and diverse offerings.

Art Galleries

San Francisco is home to an impressive array of art galleries that reflect the city's rich cultural heritage and contemporary vibrancy. These galleries showcase a wide variety of artworks, from traditional pieces to cutting-edge installations. Here's a look at some of the key art galleries in San Francisco, providing a well-rounded guide for visitors and art enthusiasts alike.

111 Minna Gallery

111 Minna Gallery, located at 111 Minna Street in downtown San Francisco, is a dynamic space that doubles as a bar and event venue by night. Known for its edgy and contemporary exhibitions, 111 Minna has been a staple in the art and nightlife scene since 1993. The gallery features works by local and international artists and hosts a variety of events, making it a social and accessible space for art lovers. It is easily reachable from most downtown hotels, and its operating hours vary depending on events.

San Francisco Museum of Modern Art (SFMOMA)

SFMOMA, located at 151 Third Street, is one of the largest modern and contemporary art museums in the United States. The museum is renowned for its extensive collection and innovative exhibitions. Visitors can expect to see works by artists such as Andy Warhol, Jackson Pollock, and Gerhard Richter, along with rotating special exhibits. SFMOMA is open Monday to Tuesday from 10:00 AM to 5:00 PM, Thursday from 1:00 PM to 8:00 PM, and Friday to Sunday from 10:00 AM to 5:00 PM. It is closed on Wednesdays. Admission fees apply, but free days are available for Bay Area residents on the first Thursday of each month.

Hosfelt Gallery

Hosfelt Gallery, located at 260 Utah Street in the DoReMi (Dogpatch, Potrero Hill, and Mission) area, specializes in showcasing contemporary art by emerging and mid-career artists. Founded in 1996, the gallery features a diverse range of mediums including painting, sculpture, and digital art. The space is known for its intellectual rigor and for nurturing the careers of internationally-renowned artists. The gallery is open Tuesday to Saturday from 10:30 AM to 5:30 PM, offering a welcoming environment for serious collectors and casual visitors alike.

Jessica Silverman Gallery

Jessica Silverman Gallery, situated at 621 Grant Avenue in Chinatown, is internationally recognized for its curated exhibitions that highlight artists relevant to contemporary culture. Since its inception, the gallery has supported a diverse roster of artists whose works have been acquired by prestigious institutions worldwide. The gallery's innovative programming includes paintings, sculptures, and digital media, often addressing themes of identity, politics, and social change. The gallery is open Tuesday to Saturday from 11:00 AM to 6:00 PM.

Minnesota Street Project

Located in the Dogpatch neighborhood, the Minnesota Street Project is a collaborative space that houses multiple galleries under one roof, including Altman Siegel Gallery, Rena Bransten Gallery, and more. This innovative project was designed to support the local art community by providing affordable spaces for artists and galleries. The complex is open Tuesday to Saturday from 11:00 AM to 6:00 PM, offering visitors a chance to explore a wide variety of contemporary artworks in a single visit. The project often hosts openings, talks, and other events that foster community engagement and artistic dialogue.

Catharine Clark Gallery

Catharine Clark Gallery, located at 248 Utah Street, focuses on contemporary art, particularly experimental video and digital media. Established in 1991, it was the first gallery in San Francisco to have a dedicated media room. The gallery represents artists who engage with challenging social and political issues through their work. Open Tuesday to Saturday from 11:00 AM to 6:00 PM, the gallery provides a platform for provocative and thought-provoking exhibitions.

When visiting San Francisco's art galleries, it's essential to plan ahead. Many galleries have varying hours and may host special events, so checking their websites for the latest information is advisable. Dress comfortably, and bring a notebook or a smartphone to jot down your thoughts or take pictures of favorite pieces (if permitted). Many galleries are within walking distance of public transportation, making it easy to include multiple visits in a single outing. Whether you are a seasoned art enthusiast or a curious visitor, San Francisco's art galleries offer a rich and engaging cultural experience.

These art galleries, among others, make San Francisco a vibrant hub for contemporary art, offering diverse and enriching experiences for all visitors.

Historic Sites and Landmarks

San Francisco is a city steeped in history, with numerous landmarks and historic sites that offer a glimpse into its rich past. These sites not only highlight the city's architectural and cultural heritage but also provide engaging experiences for visitors. Here's a look at some of San Francisco's most significant historic landmarks.

Golden Gate Bridge

The Golden Gate Bridge is one of the most iconic landmarks in San Francisco, renowned for its striking Art Deco design and vibrant International Orange color. Completed in 1937, this suspension bridge spans 1.7 miles across the Golden Gate Strait, connecting San Francisco to Marin County. Located at Fort Point, the bridge offers breathtaking views of the Pacific Ocean and the bay. Visitors can walk or bike across the bridge, and guided tours are available to learn about its history and engineering. The Golden Gate Bridge is open 24 hours, but the best time to visit is during sunrise or sunset for stunning views and fewer crowds. Expect a chilly breeze, so dress in layers. Parking is available, but public transportation via MUNI and Golden Gate Transit buses is recommended due to limited spaces.

Alcatraz Island

Alcatraz Island, situated in the middle of San Francisco Bay, was once home to the notorious federal prison that housed infamous criminals like Al Capone and Robert

Stroud. Today, it's a compelling historic site managed by the National Park Service. Visitors can take a ferry from Pier 33 Alcatraz Landing to the island, where they can explore the prison cells, solitary confinement, and guardhouses. The island also features exhibits on its history and the American Indian occupation of 1969. Alcatraz is open daily, with ferry rides starting as early as 9:00 AM. It's advisable to book tickets in advance as they often sell out. Dress warmly, as the island can be windy and cold, and wear comfortable shoes for walking. Audio tours are included with the ticket, providing a detailed and immersive experience.

Fisherman's Wharf

Fisherman's Wharf is a lively waterfront area known for its seafood restaurants, shops, and attractions. It offers a deep dive into San Francisco's maritime history. Key attractions include Pier 39, where you can watch sea lions basking in the sun, and the San Francisco Maritime National Historical Park, which features historic ships. The wharf is also home to Ghirardelli Square, where visitors can indulge in delicious chocolates and enjoy various dining options. Open year-round, Fisherman's Wharf is easily accessible via the F-Market & Wharves streetcar or multiple MUNI bus lines. Dress in layers to accommodate the changing weather and bring a camera to capture the picturesque waterfront views.

The Painted Ladies

The Painted Ladies are a row of colorful Victorian houses located in the Alamo Square neighborhood, offering a picturesque glimpse into San Francisco's architectural past. These houses are famous for their ornate details and vibrant colors, often featured in films and TV shows. Visitors can enjoy a leisurely stroll around Alamo Square Park, which provides a perfect vantage point for photographs, especially at dusk when the houses are bathed in golden light. The Painted Ladies are best accessed by the 21-Hayes MUNI bus line. There is no entrance fee as the houses are private residences, but the park is open to the public daily. Bring a picnic to enjoy the view and relax in the park.

Lombard Street

Lombard Street is known as the "crookedest street in the world" due to its eight sharp hairpin turns within a single block. Located in the Russian Hill neighborhood, the street is lined with beautiful gardens and offers a unique driving or walking experience. Visitors often come to navigate the twists and turns or to take photos of the steep, winding road against the backdrop of the city. The best way to reach Lombard Street is by taking the Powell-Hyde cable car, which stops at the top of the street. It's open to visitors year-round, and there is no admission fee. Wear comfortable shoes if you plan to walk, and be mindful of the traffic if you choose to drive down.

The Ferry Building

The Ferry Building, located at the foot of Market Street on the Embarcadero, is a historic transportation hub turned food hall. Built in 1898, it now houses a variety of artisanal food vendors, shops, and restaurants, and hosts a renowned farmers market three times a week. The building's clock tower and Beaux-Arts architecture make it a landmark. Open daily from 10:00 AM to 6:00 PM, the Ferry Building is easily accessible via the Embarcadero BART Station or the F-Market & Wharves streetcar. Bring an appetite and some cash for the farmers market, and enjoy waterfront views as you sample local delicacies.

Ghirardelli Square

Ghirardelli Square, a former chocolate factory, has been transformed into a public square filled with shops, dining spots, and entertainment options. Located at 900 North Point Street, it's famous for its Ghirardelli Chocolate Experience, where visitors can sample and purchase a variety of chocolates. The square also features mini golf, boutiques, and restaurants, making it a family-friendly destination. Open daily from 10:00 AM to 9:00 PM, Ghirardelli Square is accessible via the Powell-Hyde cable car or the 19-Polk MUNI bus line. Enjoy some chocolate treats, shop for souvenirs, and take in the historic ambiance of this beautifully preserved site.

San Francisco's historic sites and landmarks offer a rich tapestry of experiences, each contributing to the city's unique charm and historical significance. These landmarks provide unforgettable insights into the city's storied past.

Religious and Spiritual Sites

San Francisco's religious and spiritual sites offer a deep dive into the city's diverse cultural and spiritual history, serving as both places of worship and significant cultural landmarks.

Grace Cathedral

Grace Cathedral on Nob Hill is a Gothic Revival masterpiece known for its stunning architecture, "Gates of Paradise" replica doors, and two labyrinths for meditation. The cathedral offers a variety of cultural and community events, including yoga on the labyrinth. It's open daily, and admission for self-guided tours costs around $12 for adults. Dress in layers due to the cool interior and bring a camera to capture the beautiful stained glass windows.

Mission Dolores

Mission Dolores, the oldest surviving structure in San Francisco, provides a rich historical context about the Spanish missions' role in California's development. Located on Dolores Street, the mission includes the original adobe church, a newer basilica, and a serene cemetery. It's accessible via the J-Church MUNI line, open daily, and admission costs $7 for adults. The tranquil gardens and cemetery offer a peaceful retreat and a place for quiet reflection.

Old Saint Mary's Cathedral

Old Saint Mary's Cathedral, built in 1854 and located in Chinatown, survived the 1906 earthquake and continues to be a central place of worship and community activities. The Gothic Revival cathedral features stunning stained glass windows and historical artefacts. It's open daily and free to visit, though donations are welcome. Attending a mass or service can provide a deeper experience of the cathedral's spiritual ambiance.

Congregation Emanu-El

Congregation Emanu-El, near the Presidio, is one of the oldest and most architecturally significant synagogues in the United States. The Byzantine-revival building features a stunning domed sanctuary and hosts various cultural and religious events. It's accessible via the 1-California and 38-Geary MUNI bus lines and is open during regular services and by appointment. Donations are appreciated, and public tours or events are recommended for a comprehensive visit.

Tin How Temple

Tin How Temple, situated in Chinatown, is one of the oldest Taoist temples in the United States. Dedicated to the Chinese sea goddess Mazu, the temple is known for its ornate altars, incense-filled air, and serene atmosphere. It's open daily, free to visit, and located a short walk from the Powell Street BART station. Visitors should be respectful of worshippers, and photography is generally not allowed inside the temple.

These religious and spiritual sites in San Francisco provide a rich cultural heritage and serene places for reflection.

San Francisco's cultural experiences offer an unparalleled opportunity to delve into the rich history and diverse traditions of the city. Each landmark, festival, and artistic venue provides a unique window into the community, creating memorable and enriching experiences for all who explore them. The city's dedication to preserving its heritage and celebrating its artistic achievements ensures that every visit is filled with discovery and inspiration.

CHAPTER 13

Day Trips

San Francisco is surrounded by an array of stunning destinations perfect for day trips, offering diverse experiences. Here are some of the best day trips.

Napa Valley

The Napa Valley, a premier wine region, is about 50 miles north of San Francisco. You can reach Napa by car via Highway 29 or the Silverado Trail, or take a guided tour that includes transportation. The valley is home to numerous wineries, like Robert Mondavi and Beringer, where you can enjoy tours and tastings. Most wineries operate daily from 10:00 a.m. to 5:00 p.m., with tasting fees ranging from $20 to $50. Beyond wine, Napa offers hot-air balloon rides, gourmet dining, and luxurious spas. Be sure to wear comfortable shoes for exploring vineyards and bring a camera to capture the beautiful landscapes.

Sonoma

Adjacent to Napa, Sonoma is another celebrated wine region known for its charming town square and historical landmarks. The drive to Sonoma takes about an hour via Highway 101. Sonoma Plaza, the heart of the town, is surrounded by tasting rooms, boutiques, and restaurants. Key attractions include the Sonoma State

Historic Park and several renowned wineries, such as Buena Vista Winery. Sonoma's laid-back atmosphere makes it ideal for a relaxing day trip. Wineries generally charge $15 to $40 for tastings and are open from 10:00 a.m. to 5:00 p.m. Dress casually, and bring a hat and sunscreen for sunny days.

Muir Woods National Monument

Muir Woods National Monument, famous for its ancient coastal redwoods, is located 16 miles north of San Francisco. To get there, drive across the Golden Gate Bridge and follow signs for Highway 101 to Mill Valley. The park is open daily from 8:00 a.m. to sunset, with an entrance fee of $15 for adults. Parking is limited, so early arrival or shuttle service from Sausalito is recommended. The main trail is a 2-mile loop, perfect for a peaceful walk among towering trees. Wear layered clothing and comfortable hiking shoes, and bring water and snacks. The visitor centre and café offer additional amenities.

Sausalito

Just across the Golden Gate Bridge, Sausalito is a picturesque waterfront town accessible by car, bike, or ferry. The ferry from the Ferry Building, or Pier 41, offers stunning views of the bay. Sausalito's streets are lined with boutiques, art galleries, and waterfront restaurants. Attractions include the Bay Area Discovery Museum and the Marine Mammal Center. The town is perfect for leisurely exploration, with most shops and attractions open daily from 10:00 a.m. to 6:00 p.m.

Comfortable walking shoes and a camera are essentials for this scenic and relaxed outing.

Half Moon Bay

Half Moon Bay, located 30 miles south of San Francisco along Highway 1, is known for its stunning coastal scenery and outdoor activities. The drive along Highway 1 offers breathtaking ocean views. Popular activities include visiting beaches like Half Moon Bay State Beach and Mavericks Beach, hiking the Coastal Trail, and exploring the historic downtown with its shops and restaurants. The town is open year-round, with most attractions open from 10:00 a.m. to 5:00 p.m. Dress in layers and bring a picnic for a beachside meal, or opt for whale-watching tours and horseback riding.

Monterey and Carmel

Monterey and Carmel, located about 120 miles south of San Francisco, offer a blend of natural beauty and cultural attractions. The drive along Highway 1, known as the Pacific Coast Highway, is a highlight in itself. In Monterey, visit the famous Monterey Bay Aquarium and explore Cannery Row. Carmel-by-the-Sea, known for its charming village and art galleries, is perfect for strolling and shopping. Both towns have numerous dining options and scenic spots like the 17-Mile Drive. Plan for a full-day trip, with most attractions open from 10:00 a.m. to 5:00 p.m. Bring a camera, wear comfortable shoes, and prepare for a mix of activities, from beachcombing to gallery hopping.

Point Reyes National Seashore

Point Reyes National Seashore, about 40 miles northwest of San Francisco, is a stunning coastal preserve offering rugged beauty and diverse wildlife. To get there, take Highway 1 north to Point Reyes Station. The park is open daily from sunrise to sunset and has no entrance fee. Activities include hiking, wildlife viewing, and exploring the historic Point Reyes Lighthouse. Dress in layers as the weather can change rapidly, and bring binoculars for bird watching and spotting marine life. The visitor centre provides maps and information about trails and park history.

These day trips from San Francisco provide a variety of experiences, from wine tasting in world-renowned regions to exploring majestic redwoods and picturesque coastal towns. Each destination offers unique attractions and activities that cater to different interests, making them perfect escapes from the city's bustling atmosphere.

PRACTICAL INFORMATION AND TIPS

San Francisco is a captivating destination with a rich cultural tapestry and an array of attractions that cater to diverse interests. To ensure a smooth and enjoyable visit, here is detailed practical information covering various essential aspects.

Safety Tips

San Francisco is generally safe for tourists, but like any major city, it's important to stay vigilant. Petty crimes such as pickpocketing can occur in crowded areas and on public transportation, so keep an eye on your belongings. Avoid displaying valuables and be cautious in less-populated areas, especially at night. Certain neighbourhoods, like the Tenderloin, are known for higher crime rates and should be approached with caution, particularly after dark. Always be aware of your surroundings and trust your instincts. For real-time safety updates, local news sources or police advisories can be useful.

Health and Medical Services

San Francisco offers high-quality healthcare services, with numerous hospitals and clinics available. Major hospitals include UCSF Medical Centre and California Pacific Medical Center. Pharmacies are plentiful, with many open 24 hours a day. It's advisable to have travel insurance that covers medical expenses, including any necessary emergency care. In cases of minor health issues, urgent care clinics are a convenient option. The city also has excellent emergency services, with ambulances and paramedics on standby for critical situations.

Local Etiquette and Customs

San Francisco is known for its progressive and inclusive culture. Respect for diversity and personal freedoms is paramount, and visitors are expected to be open-minded and courteous. Tipping is customary in restaurants, bars, and for services such as taxis and hairdressers, with the standard being 15-20% of the total bill. Smoking is prohibited in most public places, including parks, restaurants, and bars. Recycling and composting are strongly encouraged, with many businesses and public spaces having designated bins for waste sorting.

Language

English is the primary language spoken in San Francisco. Given the city's multicultural population, you might also hear Spanish, Chinese, Tagalog, and other languages. It's helpful to know a few basic phrases in English. Most residents are accustomed to tourists and are generally friendly and willing to help with directions and recommendations.

Religion

San Francisco is home to a diverse array of religious practices and places of worship. Major religious sites include Grace Cathedral, a prominent Episcopal church; Mission Dolores, a historic Catholic mission; and Congregation Emanu-El, one of the oldest synagogues in the U.S. Additionally, there are many Buddhist temples, Hindu temples, and mosques throughout the city. Visitors are welcome at most religious sites, but it's important to be respectful of worshippers and follow any specific dress codes or customs.

Internet and Communication

San Francisco has excellent internet coverage, with free Wi-Fi available in many public places, including parks, libraries, and cafes. Most hotels and accommodations offer complimentary Wi-Fi. Mobile phone coverage is extensive, and purchasing a local SIM card can be cost-effective for international visitors who need to stay connected. Major carriers like AT&T, Verizon, and T-Mobile provide reliable service throughout the city.

Accessibility

San Francisco is committed to accessibility, with many public buildings, attractions, and transportation options accommodating those with disabilities. BART and MUNI systems are equipped with elevators and accessible platforms. Major attractions like the Golden Gate Bridge, Alcatraz Island, and the San Francisco Museum of Modern Art (SFMOMA) offer accessible facilities and services. When booking accommodations, it's best to inquire about accessibility features to ensure a comfortable stay. The city also offers programmes and resources to assist visitors with disabilities.

Currency Exchange and Banking

The official currency is the US dollar (USD). Credit and debit cards are widely accepted, though it's useful to carry some cash for small purchases or in areas where card facilities might not be available. ATMs are plentiful, and most accept international cards. Banking hours are typically Monday to Friday, with some branches open on Saturdays. Currency exchange services are available at airports, major banks, and specialised currency exchange offices. For the best exchange rates, it's advisable to use ATMs or bank services rather than airport kiosks.

Emergency Contacts

In case of emergency, dial 911 for police, fire, or medical assistance. For non-emergencies, the San Francisco Police Department can be reached at 415-553-0123. It's a good idea to note down the contact details of your country's embassy or consulate in case you need assistance. Many embassies and consulates are located in the nearby city of San Francisco, providing support and services to international visitors.

General Tips

San Francisco's weather can be unpredictable, so packing layers is essential to staying comfortable throughout the day. Popular attractions like Alcatraz Island often require advance bookings, especially during peak tourist seasons. Using public transport is often more convenient than driving due to the city's traffic and limited parking. Staying informed through local news and weather updates is also helpful, particularly if planning outdoor activities. Participating in the city's recycling and composting programmes helps maintain its commitment to sustainability. Lastly, keeping a friendly and open attitude will enhance your experience as you explore this dynamic and diverse city.

San Francisco offers a rich array of experiences and amenities, making it a fantastic destination for travelers. With this practical information, you'll be well-prepared to navigate the city and enjoy all it has to offer.

BONUS

A 4-Day Itinerary for Seeing San Francisco

Day 1

Morning

Start your day early with a visit to the iconic Golden Gate Bridge. Arrive at the Golden Gate Bridge Welcome Centre, where you can learn about the bridge's history and construction. Walk or bike across the bridge to enjoy stunning views of San Francisco Bay and the Pacific Ocean.

Next, head to the Presidio, a historic park located at the southern end of the Golden Gate Bridge. Explore its trails, visit the Presidio Officers' Club museum, and relax at Crissy Field, a scenic waterfront area perfect for a leisurely walk or picnic.

Lunch

Make your way to the Ferry Building Marketplace for lunch. This historic building on the Embarcadero houses an array of gourmet food vendors, offering everything from artisanal cheeses to fresh oysters. Enjoy your meal with views of the Bay Bridge.

Afternoon

After lunch, catch a ferry to Alcatraz Island from Pier 33. The island, once a federal prison, is now a fascinating historical site managed by the National Park Service. The ferry ride takes about 15 minutes, and the audio tour provides a compelling narrative of the prison's history and famous inmates. Be sure to book tickets in advance, as tours often sell out.

Evening

Return to the mainland and head to North Beach, San Francisco's Italian district. Stroll through the lively neighbourhood, visit the historic City Lights Bookstore, and climb the Filbert Steps to Coit Tower. From the top of Coit Tower, you'll get panoramic views of the city and the bay, making it a perfect spot for sunset.

Day 2

Morning

Begin your day at Golden Gate Park, a sprawling urban oasis. Visit the California Academy of Sciences, which houses an aquarium, planetarium, and natural history museum. Then, explore the Japanese Tea Garden, a tranquil spot with beautiful landscaping and traditional tea ceremonies.

Lunch

Head to the nearby Haight-Ashbury neighbourhood for lunch. This area, famous for its role in the 1960s counterculture movement, offers eclectic dining options, vintage shops, and colourful street art. Grab a bite at one of the local cafes or diners.

Afternoon

After lunch, take a short drive or public transport to the Mission District. Visit the Mission Dolores, the oldest surviving structure in San Francisco. Spend the afternoon exploring the vibrant murals along Clarion Alley and Balmy Alley, which reflect the neighborhood's rich cultural heritage.

Evening

Stay in the Mission District for dinner. The area is known for its fantastic Mexican food, so try a burrito from a local favorite like La Taqueria or El Farolito. Afterwards, enjoy a cocktail at one of the district's trendy bars or lounges.

Day 3

Morning

Start your day with a visit to Twin Peaks for breathtaking views of the entire city. Arrive early to avoid the crowds and capture the morning light over San Francisco's skyline.

Late Morning

Head to Union Square for some shopping. This central hub is surrounded by high-end retailers, department stores, and boutique shops. Don't miss the chance to explore the nearby Maiden Lane, a charming pedestrian street with more shops and cafes.

Lunch

Walk to Chinatown, one of the oldest and largest Chinese communities outside Asia. Enjoy a dim sum lunch at a popular spot like City View Restaurant or Yank Sing. After lunch, wander through the bustling streets, visit the Golden Gate Fortune Cookie Factory, and explore the historic Tin How Temple.

Afternoon

Hop on a cable car for a ride to Fisherman's Wharf. Explore the wharf's attractions, including Pier 39, where you can watch sea lions basking in the sun. Visit the Aquarium of the Bay or take a cruise around the bay for close-up views of the Golden Gate Bridge and Alcatraz Island.

Evening

End your day with a seafood dinner at Fisherman's Wharf. Restaurants like Scoma's and Alioto's offer fresh seafood and bay views. After dinner, take a leisurely stroll along the waterfront.

Day 4

Morning

Set out early for a day trip to Napa Valley, about an hour's drive from San Francisco. Start your visit with a tour and tasting at one of the many renowned wineries, such as Robert Mondavi or Domaine Carneros. Enjoy the scenic drive through rolling vineyards and picturesque landscapes.

Lunch

Head to the town of Yountville for lunch. Bouchon Bakery offers delicious pastries and sandwiches, while nearby restaurants like Bistro Jeanty provide classic French cuisine. Stroll through the town's art galleries and boutique shops after your meal.

Afternoon

Drive to Sonoma, another celebrated wine region. Visit the Sonoma Plaza, surrounded by tasting rooms, shops, and restaurants. Tour one of the local wineries, such as Buena Vista Winery or Chateau St. Jean, and enjoy a tasting. The relaxed atmosphere and beautiful surroundings make for a perfect afternoon.

Evening

Return to San Francisco in the evening. For your last dinner in the city, consider dining in one of the diverse neighbourhoods you may have missed earlier, such as the Marina District or the Financial District, where you'll find a variety of dining options to suit any taste.

CONCLUSION

As your journey in San Francisco draws to a close, taking time to reflect on your experiences can deepen your appreciation of the city. San Francisco, with its eclectic neighbourhoods, iconic landmarks, and diverse culture, likely provided countless memorable moments. Reflecting on these experiences not only cements them in your memory but also offers valuable insights that can enhance future travels.

To ensure your departure is as smooth as your stay, confirm your travel arrangements well in advance. Double-check your flight details, arrange transportation to the airport, and consider the local traffic patterns. San Francisco International Airport (SFO) is well-connected, but arriving early is advisable, particularly during peak travel seasons, to avoid any last-minute stress.

If you've acquired souvenirs during your stay, ensure they are well-packed and comply with airline regulations and customs laws, both in the U.S. and your home country. Some items, like certain food products or cultural artefacts, might have restrictions or require special handling, so it's important to check the latest customs regulations to ensure all your souvenirs are legal to export.

Handling leftover U.S. dollars can be straightforward; you might want to exchange some back into your home currency before leaving, although keeping some cash for last-minute purchases or emergencies is also wise.

Currency exchange counters at the airport offer competitive rates, but you might get better deals at local exchange services in town.

Take some time to journal or compile your photos. This not only helps in preserving your memories but can also assist friends and family who may be planning a trip to San Francisco. Reflect on what you enjoyed most, any cultural insights you gained, and what you might do differently next time. Sharing these reflections on platforms like TripAdvisor, Google Reviews, or personal blogs can be incredibly helpful for other travellers and local businesses.

On your last day, try to relax and soak up as much of San Francisco as you can. Enjoy a final meal at one of the city's renowned restaurants, take a leisurely stroll along the waterfront, or visit a favourite spot one last time. These final moments often provide the perfect end to an incredible journey, offering a chance to savour the city's unique ambiance.

When it's time to leave, ensure you have all your belongings, travel documents, and any necessary health certifications. At the airport, as you wait for your flight, it's a good moment to reflect on your journey and the ways it has enriched your life. Think about the vibrant neighbourhoods you explored, the diverse culinary delights you savoured, and the iconic landmarks you visited. These moments are not just memories, but treasures that will inspire and fuel your wanderlust for years to come.

As you turn the last page of this chapter in San Francisco, take a moment to appreciate how travel enriches our lives, broadens our perspectives, and connects us to the heartbeat of diverse cultures. Keep your spirit of discovery alive, and let the memories of San Francisco guide you gently back to this unique city by the bay. Safe travels, and may San Francisco leave a lasting impression in your heart and mind.

EVELYN BLAIR.

Printed in Great Britain
by Amazon